RAISING PARENTS

The Journey of Caregiving Amid Perilous Times

By C. M. Montclair

D P Book Publishing

Copyright © 2024 by C. M. Montclair

Visit the author's website at www.dppublishing.club

All rights reserved.

No part of this publication may be reproduced, distributed, or transmitted in any form or by any means, including photocopying, recording, or other electronic or mechanical methods, without the prior written permission of the publisher, except as permitted by U.S. copyright law. For permission requests, contact raisingparentsbook@dppublishing.club

ISBN 979-8-9904425-0-4 (print)

For privacy reasons, some names, locations, and dates may have been changed.

Book Cover by VeryMuchSo.Agency

Back Cover headshot by Shuneil Gadson

1st edition 2024 | Printed in the U.S.A.

Published by D P Book Publishing
Huntsville, AL
www.dppublishing.club

Table of Contents

Preface 6
Chapter 1: And So it Begins 9
Chapter 2: What's happening?! 19
Chapter 3: Sigh 28
Chapter 4: The Getaway 37
Chapter 5: I'm leaving! 47
Chapter 6: Well, This is New! 62
Chapter 7: What Now?? 68
Chapter 8: Blessings Can't Be Blocked 79
Chapter 9: Coordination, please! 86
Chapter 10: I Want to Buy a House! 101
Chapter 11: The New Normal 114
Chapter 12: The Aftermath 124
Chapter 13: Who are you convincing? 148
Chapter 14: So Let It Be Written, So Let It Be Done 162
RESOURCES 172

To Mom and Dad,

You did a good job raising your daughters.

Acknowledgements

I must acknowledge the impactful people and organizations in my life who have helped me to navigate through my parents' illnesses. Even though I'm a quiet and private person, they have greatly influenced my life and emotional path.

To Rev. Dr. Julius R Scruggs who taught me about God's word, God's faithfulness, how to pray, and how to trust while he pastored First Missionary Baptist Church in Huntsville, Alabama. Pastor Scruggs took the time to unselfishly visit my father and mother while they were sick in the hospital and at home. Even during his time as President of the National Baptist Convention, He still made time to check on the well-being of my parents. He stills checks on my father to this day. **He is IMPACT**.

To First Missionary Baptist Church where the Brotherhood Chorus, Missionary Society, and Congregational Care always looked out for my father and mother. **They have EMPATHY.**

To Evell Bowie for consistently checking on my father by coming by the house to see him even to this day during his retirement. **He is COMMITMENT**.

To my sister, because we both endure our parents together and have had many days of laughter to get us through the tough times. We balance the tasks between us and still find time to live our own lives as sisters and best friends. Let's have a drink together!! **She is FAMILY**.

Preface

To be in our family, you must have thick skin. We joke all the time and engage in shenanigans every day. We turn emotions, arguments, vacations, sickness, and holidays into comedic tears of laughter. It's how we survive. Laughter has been a way of coping with situations in our family for three generations and has helped us endure the toughest issues with renewed faith.

My perspective on my parents' health throughout the years has been a blessed rollercoaster that has built my faith, hope and trust in God. This book is not a sad story, but rather it's an enlightening journey through faith where strength resides. It's a way of changing the mind from current understandings to a holistic perspective. Who else would allow someone to endure so much pain only to live through it and tell others about it. Only God! Every trial my family has been through led to a deeper faith while wholly depending on God's presence.

So be prepared to learn how to find joy in victory and be released from unnecessary stress as a caregiver.

As you read this book, you'll realize names have been omitted. The point is to connect with familial ties and understand how family relations influence our decisions and actions. Do not focus on the names but feel the relationships throughout the book. It is not about Sheila, Maryanne, Michael, John, William, or even Beverly, Natasha, and Lisa. It is about your mom, your dad, your aunt, your Husband, your Wife, your Child, your best friend, your cousin. Remember, you hardly ever say, "yeah Sheila is not doing well." Instead, you say, "yeah, my mom is not doing well." So, yes, the names have been omitted.

Also, it helps to protect the innocent.

Chapter 1: And So it Begins

Elementary School

I was a quiet little kid. I didn't say too much, but I loved to play and ride my bike around the neighborhood. I'm the youngest of two girls and my sister and I are 10 years apart. With us being 10 years apart, we were already living completely separate lives by the time I reached fifth grade. My sister was already living on her own now with her own family. We definitely didn't have anything in common at the time as she was busy starting her career, being a wife, and being a mother while I was trying to figure out which new tennis shoes I could have. I wanted to be all in her world, but we were just different at the time. I was "in her way". So, I ended up having the house and our parents to myself. Even though my sister moved out, it was still a win win for me! But I kept thinking, "Did my parents really have to wait 10 years before deciding to have me?" Like, what was the hold up?! I started to believe my sister when she said I was a MISTAKE. Ugh…. rude!

I'm introverted. Meaning I didn't like talking to my parent's friends, nor being around a bunch of people, or speaking to everyone. Being around numerous people all the time or going to a lot of back-to-back events drains my energy so I need quiet alone time to refuel. When I was younger, everyone thought I was this cute little girl and I kept wondering why people were talking to me and harassing me for hugs. Yes, they've known my parents for a long time, but they have not known me for 10 minutes. Therefore, they're all strangers! I'm introverted. It took me awhile to realize that when I was younger but came to accept and understand it more as I got older.

At my young age, I think my parents are kind of cool. Nothing too special about them, just regular parents. Mom always cooked a good meal, made sure that I presented my best self, and be articulate. "Speak up and annunciate your words, Monica!" is what she would tell me. Mom was a schoolteacher and was a firm believer that her children would be articulate and intelligent. Besides being a teacher, she always had somewhere to go because she was involved with so many things so I liked riding with her to run errands because I knew we would get something sweet to eat later. Dad usually had a joke or something clever to say. He would play outside with me all the time and show me something cool and interesting that sparked my curiosity. I loved going outside on discoveries since it expanded my imagination. My parents were regularly active in church, and they would carry me to church with them every time they went. They were always in some ministry helping with feeding the sick and shut in, singing in the choir, supporting a prayer group, or just helping with church activities. We were at church at least three days a week so I grew up not knowing what it was like to not go to church. It was a normal routine for us to be active and present in church. At this age, it did not matter to me, I just liked the snacks they had in Sunday School. I was outdoorsy so we liked getting into things to learn something new. Sister was the big sister that thoroughly enjoyed locking me out of OUR room and keeping me out of her business. She would bribe me with fresh baked brownies to keep me from blabbing about her shenanigans. Whatever I had to do to stay in her circle, I made sure to do it with a chocolate fudge brownie in my hand.

School was fun for me, especially my fifth-grade year in elementary school. I was on the safety patrol team wearing my little sash to help direct traffic. I owned that traffic lane and felt that my little arm kept the traffic flowing smoothly. I had my group of friends that I talked to and sat with at lunch, and I was in Mrs. Sawyer's class. I LOVED being in her class. It was smooth, fun, and comfortable! That was life back then! Easy living, minimal worries besides not getting new toys or the next scratch on my knee. I loved being outside all day long to go exploring. Whether it was with friends or by myself, I would stay outside until the streetlights came on. I would get in trouble every now and then for going too far from the house, which was going two streets over. Healthy life, good friends, and outdoor activities made life epic. Those were definitely the good old days. During elementary school, we had just moved into our new house that my dad and I found while riding bikes in the neighborhood. There was a house that was in the next neighborhood that I wanted because it was a two-story house. I learned that it was a split-level house meaning there's a bottom level where the first flight of stairs leads to the main part of the house and a second flight of stairs that leads to the bedrooms. I thought it was fun to have two flights of stairs to play on and slide down. So, I convinced my parents to get the house mainly for the stairs so I can run up and down them to my own bedroom. I enjoyed having my own bedroom and I didn't have to share one with my sister who liked locking me out. I loved running up and down the stairs to my room to do my little homework and watch my favorite shows. Life was easy! I mean, come on…I was 10 years old. It was good living. Easy living….

Then out of the blue my Mom got sick. Not like a cold sick, but SICK sick. It seemed like it came out of nowhere because I don't remember her being weak or ill or anything. She started to have constant symptoms and went to the doctor a few times about it until finally she found out she was diagnosed with breast cancer.

BREAST CANCER? What is that? Breast get sick? How do you wake up and have it? What did she eat! My family was pretty healthy for the most part before this happened, so it was a bit of a shocker.

My little self had the nerve to look down inside my shirt to see if I had breast cancer. Like can I get it before my boobs come in? Selfishly and ignorantly, I kept my distance from my mom for a couple of days because I didn't want to "catch" her cancer. Apparently, I thought it was something like cooties at the time. Keep in mind that I was 10 years old.

At that age I had no idea what that meant, but I knew it was a bad sickness. I quickly learned that cancer was an attack on cells and not just a temporary virus. We went to numerous doctor's appointments and got second opinions about what cancer is and the type of treatment that was needed.

I learned about chemotherapy treatment, radiation, and the side effects that would be experienced while diminishing the spread of cancer. Chemotherapy basically kills off the bad cancer cells so that the good cells can repair damage that was done in the body. It's a very rigorous process that drains your energy, makes you very nauseous, and strips all the hair from you. That was my perspective of it at my young age. Chemo just seemed so harsh on the body and required multiple sessions to complete the process. It literally drains life out of you just to get your health back to normal. Learning about the process, my mother wanted to take herbal supplements instead of chemo (which we have named the "red devil"), for obvious reasons. She felt that a natural solution was more realistic and less damaging to her body, but my father tried to convince her on how the chemo and the science would help her. He wanted her to trust the process and medical advancements to beat this thing, instead of giving up. I remember them talking about it and how it would save her life and she just wasn't having it. She wanted to live without struggling and being sick. But in my mind, all I kept thinking was that she doesn't want to be here with US?! She'd rather take a chance on shortening her life and leave us down here along……RUDE! At that time, we thought that natural remedies weren't strong enough to beat such an aggressive cancer. She went through getting advice from another doctor just to be sure this was all true, all a reality. I remember during the first doctor's consultation, he went through the surgery process, number of treatments, side effects and recovery phase with my parents and me. He drew a sketch of her breast to show what will be cut off to remove the cancer. Dad wanted to make sure I understood everything, but also wanted to make sure I'm ok. Keep in mind, I was only 10 years old. While interrupting the doctor's explanation,

"Hey, are you ok?" asked Dad.

"Yeah" I replied. I thought was those boobs are going to bother him more than me, so I wanted to ask him "Are YOU okay?"

"Do you understand what's going on?" asked Mom.

"Yeah" again I replied with a simple answer, but on the inside, I was quietly asking myself "do YOU understand what's going on?"

Disclaimer: sometimes parents ask their children questions because they're scared too. It's a way to deflect the situation while still trying to deal with it. I feel you girl, I would be scared too!

Even though she wanted to skip the chemicals and hospitals, I'm glad she listened to Dad and took the chemo. Of course, her hair fell out and she vomited all her insides out, but she persevered. Seeing her lose her hair, lose her energy, and have a piece of her taken away changed my perspective on illness. Going through surgery, learning how to adapt to a new body, and coming home having to love yourself all over again can be hard going through breast cancer. I remember having a sleepover with one of my friends who knew about my mom being sick. When my mom's hair started falling out, she would walk around the house with a scarf on her head and my friend was trying to look under her scarf every time she walked by. My friend was trying to see if she had any hair left under there. I noticed her trying to awkwardly look under there and wanted to distract her, but I was mad that she was being nosey. I told her that she was being rude about it, and she had the nerve to tell me "My grandmother didn't want me to spend the night because she said I could catch cancer." WHY WOULD SHE SAY THAT! Who spends the night at a friend's house just to snoop around and try to figure out if their mom's hair was gone?! RUDE!! Therefore, I never invited her back and barely talked to her after that. So now I must deal with ignorant people too?! UGH!

My mom was weak enough to let breast cancer affect her, but strong enough to overcome it and start taking responsibility. Her right breast was removed so I had to remember that the right side of her body was no longer the chill side. Just can't lay on that arm anymore because that's where they had to remove her breast. All I could remember was the doctor saying, "remove the breast, remove the cancer." At that age, cancer to me was a real dramatic way of resetting the body through the most gruesome way.

My attitude changed after that. I became quieter and more concerned with how cancer happens. Where does it come from? Am I next? If I do all my work and get good grades, will it skip me? Could good behavior keep me from inheriting cancer? In Mrs. Sawyer's class I wasn't as happy anymore because I was too worried about my mom's life instead of living life. How many years does my mom have with us? How many years do I have with her?

By the time I'm preparing to enter middle school, Mom had overcome breast cancer, survived chemo, and has returned to work as a special education teacher. She's learned about special bras to purchase to make your breast look even and different wigs you can wear while you wait for your hair to come back. She found support groups, medicines and comforting tactics to help improve the recovery time. She felt self-conscious about having one breast and how it changed her body image, but she wouldn't let that overshadow who she was. It took some time, but she got used to her new body and found clothing that made her feel confident again. As a family, we were able to endure that battle and enjoy life again.

Whew! Back to normal.

Consider it pure joy, my brothers and sisters, whenever you face trials of many kinds, because you know that the testing of your faith produces perseverance. Let perseverance finish its work so that you may be mature and complete, not lacking anything. James 1:2-4 NIV

Sometimes the Lord takes you through trials because he needs to strengthen you and build your faith. He knows you can live with a thorn in your flesh and lets you live with a thorn in your flesh to still praise him.

People, it is important that we check on our bodies regularly. We're the only ones using our bodies every hour of every day. Pay attention to changes, things that feel weird, or physical behaviors that seem to be new. I don't mean just the knees crackling because they're going to do that anyway. That's called the warmup phase. I'm talking about feelings of tiredness, discomfort, stomach pains, lumps, and mood changes. These are signs that your body wants you to pay attention to.

So, schedule your mammogram today. Don't wait! We must trust that God has power to use the doctors and specialists whom He blessed to fix a problem.

I would rather want to know what's wrong early than to miss out on healing solutions later.

Chapter 2: What's happening?!

So now I'm in middle school. We're back to normal and we don't have to call the doctor's office and hospital our home anymore. Both parents are working, and we go through the usual life problems: car trouble, A/C going out, and rising cost of living. Normal stuff I didn't have to worry about. During this time, Mom and Dad are working full-time trying to make ends meet. I'm in the band at middle school now playing the clarinet and going through the usual middle school foolishness. I have my same set of friends and made a few more. Still the quiet one but learning my own style and growing into my personality. I'm in my tom boyish stage so big hoodies, loose jeans, and big t-shirts were my thing. It kind of hid the fact that I was super skinny. Like 90lbs when wet kind of skinny. My mom used to always say "People are going to think I don't feed you. We have to get you some vitamins." I eat, just not a lot and I love to snack, but mainly on fruits and vegetables. So, I would wear bigger clothes to sort of hide my skinny and plus they were very comfortable. Middle school was interesting because children notice differences in other people quickly. Like my big lips! You'll earn some of the cruelest nicknames in middle school, but it didn't faze me. Yeah, I have big lips, but so what! I let the jokes go in one ear and out the other. I was just chilling in middle school trying to get the first chair in band while playing the clarinet and learning how to get through math. I was great at English, but horrible at Math. On the other hand, I enjoyed the field trips we went on in middle school like the Black History Museum; Native American History Museum; Six Flags over Georgia; the aquarium; and the zoo. My dad would always volunteer to chaperone the field trips whenever he could. He was like the cool Dad that all my friends would like to hang around with. He had all the jokes and encouraging words without making kids feel dumb or disliked. Dad worked hard to make sure we had what we needed in the house and to make sure we were loved. He's pretty healthy and hasn't had too many sicknesses outside the usual common cold.

All of a sudden, Dad's back starts randomly hurting. First, it starts off as a little discomfort, maybe from sleeping wrong or straining it the wrong way. Not sure why it's hurting so he continues to go to work in pain. Eventually the pain got so bad that he could barely walk or even ride in a car, especially going across rough roads. His back pain would make him feel each bump in the road and he had to raise himself off the seat just to avoid the rockiness. Keep in mind, mom's driving is horrible. She had to drive more since Dad's back was causing him so much pain and every time she would drive, that is when Mom runs over every speed bump, pothole and jumps every curb. Dad said,

"Do you have to hit EVERY bump in the road? You know, you can avoid those since I'm having to adjust every time you hit a bump."

Mom would say, "Do you want to drive?"

"Can we just get there?!" was always Dad's reply.

Dad's back pain changed how he walked, how he sat, his energy, but somehow, he kept a smile on his face. I would see him go to work walking in the door in so much pain and still work a full 8-hour shift. He would come home and just lay down to get some sort of relief. One night, his back hurt so badly, he couldn't lie in the bed and only had relief on the floor. No pillows, no air mattress, no nothing. Just a blanket and the floor. To me it looked very uncomfortable, but for him it was a bit of a relief. The next morning comes, and he cannot get off the floor. He was stuck lying flat on the floor. Whenever there's a bad situation, my dad always starts it with "Ok, we've got a situation." We had to figure out several ways to get him off the floor without causing more back pain. He wasn't close enough to the bed to use it as leverage to pull up on, plus that would've caused him more pain. We brainstormed a few techniques like we were corporate heist men when we eventually decided to try the pulley system. The plan was to loop a rope through a chair and use my weight as leverage so he could pull himself up and BOOM! He'll be off the floor. Mind you I was only 90 lbs. at the time so guess what happened when he pulled the rope? The chair and I both fell! The chair was heavier than me! I fell with the chair and in disappointment Dad said "Ohhhh Monica. You added no weight to the chair at all. Are we feeding you?!" Hopes and dreams for that solution were gone.

Plan B: I gathered all the pillows in the house and started stuffing them next to his shoulder to help him turn onto his side. I literally found 20 pillows around the house to help him turnover. I started at his shoulder, and we would countdown until he was ready to shift again so that I could stuff more pillows under him. To make sure we communicated well, Dad would say, "Ok, I'm going to count to three, breath, then turnover so that you can stuff pillows under me. Use as many pillows as possible so I can get off the floor."

"Are you in a lot of pain?" I asked him.

"A little, but it's going to be alright. Ready?

"Ready!"

"1….2……3…. stuff, stuff, stuff!"

Every time he shifts, I would stuff a pillow under him. First, we were able to get his shoulder off the floor, then get his entire left side off the floor, and eventually get his upper back off the floor. The goal was to at least get him sitting up to pull him off the floor. Once he was able to sit up then he could use his legs to push up while I held his hands to pull him off the floor. Seven pillows, one failed plan, and three hours later he was off the floor.

"We gotta feed you", Dad said.

Then here comes Mom.

As Mom is walking back into the house she says, "What you all doing?"

(This is that moment where we've been struggling with this and help finally shows up and our first thought is "Where were YOU?")

"Nothing, just getting Dad up from the floor" I answered.

"You're just now getting off the floor??" she says.

We both give Mom the quick rundown of the scenario andsay, "Everything is good now." Dad learned very quickly that sleeping on the floor was not ideal, but his back pain is inconvenient.

No one likes restrictions and since your back controls body movement, when it hurts then the whole body is affected. I could tell he was getting frustrated with his back pain and just wanted it gone. I didn't know how I could help besides just being there for him.

Dad doesn't catch a cold too often and tries to knock it out as fast as he can. He caught a cold, and this one has him down bad. It shuts him down to where all he can do is stay in the bed and take some medicine until one night, he's upstairs asleep while Mom and I are downstairs watching TV. I faintly heard some noises but thought it was just some sounds from the TV.

"You hear that?" I asked Mom.

"No. What do you hear?"

"Sounds like yelling."

"Nope, don't hear it."

A few minutes pass and we hear this knocking sound and still assume it's nothing. We continue watching TV for a whole extra hour when Mom says, "Go check on your dad." I go upstairs to check on him and he says "FINALLY!" The man had been knocking on the bedroom wall as a signal for help for us to hear it downstairs. He had been knocking for two hours while we ignored the, at the time, obnoxious sound.

"I've been knocking for quite a while; you all didn't hear it?!" Dad said in frustration.

With an oops look on my face, I replied "Yeah we heard it just didn't know it was from you."

"I couldn't yell that loud so I thought knocking on the wall would help."

Well, now we're here for the rescue and he has been sweating like crazy. I noticed all the sweat and I yelled to Mom to quickly come upstairs. We realized he had a fever. Mom decides that we should take him to the hospital. By this time, it's 9 o'clock at night and Dad definitely doesn't feel like going to the hospital. That means he must get up, get dressed, and figure out how to get down the stairs and in the car. This is when I learned that Dad doesn't like being bothered with hospitals. The constant needle pricking, tests, nurses in and out of the room, and back and forth just makes an uncomfortable situation worse. He would rather stay home and tough it out than be bothered with the logistics of going to the hospital. He'll wait until the 11th hour before saying "Ok, I'll go." This time the trouble is how are we going to get this 175 lb. man who barely wants to walk down two flights of stairs and into the car? Mom and I stand on both sides of him and tell him to shift his weight onto us. We slowly get him out of the bed, and step by step he gets down the stairs and finally makes it to the car. His back pain quickly went from 10 to 10,000 in a matter of minutes.

Mom and I rush him to the hospital to get him checked out and thankfully my sister runs the emergency room department at the hospital so we kind of get first dibs on getting checked into a room. I mean she LITERALLY runs that emergency room!! Thank God for her because I DO NOT have the wherewithal to manage a beast like that. She's always been good at saving lives while I'm good at building a savings for life.

The doctors ran some tests and found out he has pneumonia. Based on his current condition and the level of pain in his back, the doctors ran some more tests and tried to get his fever down. They decided to keep him overnight to watch him more closely. Since it's the middle of the night, Mom and I have to decide whether we're going to stay overnight with him or head back home. I had school the next morning, but I wouldn't mind missing it for this. Eventually, we decided to go home and think about what time we'll head back to the hospital to pick him up. Here is when I find out that God let's things happen because he sees the whole picture while we're still figuring out the colors.

Our bodies talk to us daily, but we don't listen to it until it's too late. We're the only ones around our bodies 24/7 and yet we ignore or neglect it. Listening to our bodies is vital for us to improve our health and extend our days. We push through the pain and discomfort and convince ourselves it's "normal." Here's where our bodies stop whispering to us and just flat-out YELLS!

Because Dad had pneumonia, the doctors were able to find out that pneumonia was the least of his problems. It was just a way to get him to the hospital. After running a few tests, they informed us that his back pain was a result of cancer. CANCER! Multiple Myeloma kind of cancer.

Multiple myeloma is a blood cancer because it attacks plasma cells in the bone marrow. Usually, plasma cells make antibodies, but in my dad's case, his plasma cells turned into cancer cells that were raging in his body. This meant he couldn't fight off infections and his body was basically at war with itself. Not only was his body damaging itself, but it also made it harder for him to fight off external sickness, like the common cold or the flu. His back had been hurting because his spine was filled with bad bone marrow and was spreading cancer cells all over his body. Multiple myeloma started attacking his red and white blood cells that eventually weakened his immune system. Hence the pneumonia. Why in the world would there be such a thing as Multiple Myeloma? What would make your body go from normal one day to biological foolishness the next day? How does it flip the switch from good to bad? By this time, I'm growing frustrated with God because these illnesses just don't make sense to me.

Lord, you're basically coming for my mother AND my father; GOT IT! Lord, I don't know your plans, but I see what you're doing, and I don't like it!

I've learned full well that if we keep playing around with our bodies, it will shut down on us. And the timing is ALWAYS wrong!

Three times I pleaded with the Lord to take it away from me. But He said to me, "My grace is sufficient for you, for my power is made perfect in weakness." Therefore, I will boast all the more gladly about my weaknesses, so that Christ's power may rest on me.

-2 Corinthians 12:8-9

Chapter 3: Sigh

So now we're going through cancer again, but this takes a different route. This is blood cancer, which is a unique type for us. We haven't heard much about Multiple Myeloma and weren't aware of any people who had it. We just knew it affected the blood and a solution had to be implemented fast. By this time, I'm heading into high school so while I'm learning about biology in school, I'm experiencing it in my household. Being a freshman in high school, trying to figure myself out, and learning how to not be a selfish teenager was an interesting time. As a family, we had a two-year break between my mom's cancer before my dad's cancer started. Two years doesn't seem that long when it comes to healing. It goes by rather fast.

We go through the medical consultation, again, about what Multiple Myeloma is and how the oncologists are going to treat it. Remember all the fuss about stem cell therapy? I'm glad you knew because this was new to me as well. I was in high school! But now I'm about to learn the ins and outs of stem cell therapy while also learning about biology in school. Stem cell therapy is a way of treating blood cancers in a more systematic way without trying to cause too much harm to the patient's body. Stem cell therapy is a regenerative medicine where the procedure involves taking dad's blood out to separate the bad blood cells and cycling it back into his body with good blood and plasma. The goal is to harvest his stem cells from his bone marrow while he takes radiation to kill off the cancerous cells in his body. After the radiation treatment, doctors would then return his stem cells back into his body and those cells would transform into good cells that were lacking in his body. In his case, that would be his stem cells generating into new blood cells to repair and rebuild his low blood cells count. It's amazing how God didn't just create red and white blood cells, but He also created stem cells that could reproduce itself once weak areas in the body were recognized. Ain't God good!

Naturally, it took the doctors some more time to explain it to us because it sounded like a weird way of doing dialysis. Mom and I were both wondering how this was going to work. It just seemed foreign at the time. The first step was to take Dad's blood out of him to start the stem cell therapy process. I remember the doctors having to put a catheter into my dad's chest. To me, it looked like something Iron Man would have inserted in his chest; basically, my dad was Iron Man now. SWEET!

When it comes to anything dealing with the body, Dad explains it as detailed as possible. Talking about death? Yep, he's going to describe each phase of the body decomposing. Talking about animals shedding their skin? Yep, he's going to give detailed information beginning to end. Talking about a huge cut on his arm? Yep, he's going to talk about the layers of skin, the healing process and why scabs look so scabby. Dad and I talked about all the gruesome stuff, so I was barely queasy about things. He would always end the conversation with "are you ok? Just want to make sure you're not scared. It's all about understanding what's going on. Everything is going to be ok."

Understanding Multiple Myeloma and stem cell therapy took some time, so I learned how to literally take things day by day. It was more of my understanding the lesson behind the illness. Mom used to ask me all the time,

"I'm nervous throughout this process and your sister is just upside down about all this; everyone's having a hard time with this. But you, you're just calm. Just emotionless. Do you not care?"

"I care."

"So how are you so calm about all this while we're all just all over the place??"

I replied, "If Dad says it's going to be ok, then it's going to be ok."

"So that's all you needed to hear?"

"He's the one that's sick. He's the one that's in the hospital. If HE'S saying it's going to be ok, then it's going to be ok."

"Well……. I'm not like you" she says.

The good thing about me is that I have self-control of my emotions. But that's also a bad thing to have so much control of my emotions. Be mindful of the ones that can control their emotions. We're quite powerful, or what some people may think as dangerous. The person who can control their emotions can control the room.

Dad was in the hospital for a long time so the normal schedule would be school, hospital, then home. I remember waking up, going to school, then leaving school to go visit Dad in the hospital before coming back home. Mom and I did that every day during my freshman to sophomore years of high school to where it became annoying. Sometimes mundane routines create weird feelings you're not aware of until it becomes too late. The routine led to me feeling numb. Just numb. I went to school wondering when he would be able to come home, then went to the hospital wondering when I can go back to school for the distraction. Feeling numb led me to being super nonchalant. A few of my high school experiences were more like welcomed distractions than super enjoyable moments. The main things that mattered to me were just wanting Dad to get out of the hospital and be healthy so I could worry about regular high school issues instead of family health issues. Selfish? Yes. Honest? Yes. Irritated? YES! There was a time I let my irritation out when Dad was in a sanitization room. For some time, he had to be in a sanitized room to prevent the onset of Tuberculosis (TB) since his immune system was completely shot and needed protection from outside germs. Including family members. Everything that was brought into that room had to be completely covered. Doctors, nurses, food, and even fresh bed sheets had to be covered. I was highly offended! You're telling me I must wear a mask and go through a sanitizing blowing section BEFORE I can see my dad? You're restricting ME from seeing the man I've known ALL MY LIFE?! Whatever! I walked in and took the mask off and sat on his bed like normal. We started talking and Dad asked his usual questions when I noticed that he didn't finish eating his dinner for that day (probably because he's tired of hospital food by now) and didn't even touch his fruit. I love fruit so I started uncovering his fruit bowl to pick out some fruit and started to eat his grapes all in his face. His only response was "if you want them, you can eat them. Eat, eat."

My mother on the other hand, was tired of me.

"I really wish you wouldn't eat those. That fruit is for him. Plus, you need to be sitting over here by me, so you won't make him sick" she yelled at me.

"…. but I'm not sick…"

"YOU will get him sick being so close to him like that. Cover the fruit back up and leave it alone."

Dad spoke up and said "she can eat it. It won't hurt."

"But she needs to learn how to follow directions" was mom's response as I just continued to eat more grapes while they were going back and forth until Mom glanced back at me.

"PUT THE GRAPES DOWN!!" she yelled.

I gently wrapped the fruit back up all nice and neat, placed them back on the dinner tray, and firmly but quietly walked to the chair across the room to sit down.

Parents, sometimes your children are not being defiant as a sign of disrespect. They really just don't like interruptions in life that they weren't prepared for. Children are learning about the world through their own eyes and perspective, and when things don't add up based on their thinking, children act out that emotion. I wasn't mad that I was told not to eat the grapes. I was mad that I couldn't sit with my dad like I normally would at home.

Mom and Dad continue to talk, and I sit there quietly until Mom says "ok, I'm tired and still have to drive home. We're going to head home and call you tomorrow." This frustrated me again because why are we leaving so early? WE JUST GOT HERE! UGH!! We ended up saying our goodbyes, made sure Dad was ok, and started to head out. I could tell that he's tired. Not physically tired, but mentally and soulfully tired. His face shows that he's ready to feel better, get out of the hospital, get back to living again, and do what he wants to do. To me, he felt stuck, and I could feel it. But what could I do.... selfishly eat his grapes?

Mom and I headed downstairs to the hospital's cafeteria to get dinner. For some odd reason, the burgers from the hospital cafeteria grill are THE best!! I don't know what they put in them, but they have a chokehold on Mom and me. We get our made in heaven burgers with fries and sit down at a table in the cafeteria. Out of the blue, I started coughing and not like a dainty little cough. An uncontrollable cough as if I'm coughing up a lung. Of course, Mom starts fussing at me.

"See! You're probably coughing from eating those grapes. I told you not to eat them" as she continues to fuss while I'm coughing.

"You have to be more mindful around your dad because he can't take on another sickness and we can't be bringing in germs when we come to see him". I hear what she's saying, but clearly, I'm choking. She continued to fuss.

"Now you'll listen to me! I told you not to eat those grapes. You're coughing because you ate his grapes!"

I'm still coughing and now I have water in my eyes. I ended up choking on those grapes. Obviously, God wanted to give me a lashing for that too.

At the time, I thought the whole sanitization room was a way to keep me from my dad. Now that I'm older, I realize it was a way to keep him protected from us because his immune system was shot. He ended up losing a lot of weight, his skin became darker, lost his hair and had less energy while in the hospital battling cancer with stem cell therapy and radiation. Seeing physical ailments because of an internal body war is wild. I've seen the worst phases of cancer. There are things worse than death.

Mom and I kept our routine every other day. We continued to go see my dad in the hospital like clockwork. During the day, sister would check on him in between her shifts managing the emergency room while Mom was teaching at an elementary school, and I was in class. Mom would get off from work, leave the school to come pick me up from high school, then head to the hospital after getting extra clothes from the house for Dad. We'd stay there with him for a couple hours then head back home to get ready for the next day. I would help clean the house and complete my homework before starting the day over. The days we didn't go to visit him, we ended up running errands to meetings, grocery shopping, washing clothes, and preparing the house for his return. Preparing the house meant sanitizing the whole house, new linens, and organization. Days turned into weeks, and we were exhausted from all the back and forth, but Dad's strength was finally starting to come back and recover from the stem cell therapy.

We've seen the worst part of stem cell therapy and now we're preparing to experience the end stages of the procedure and its benefits. Now that radiation has killed off the cancerous cells, it's time to return the healthy cells back into Dad's body. As he's pumped with cells, it seems like his body is rejuvenated. The stem cells act like little investigators to spot weak areas in the body and whatever the body lacks that has created a weakness, stem cells work to repair those damaged areas. Stem cells can become skin, brain, red blood cells, etc. to get the body back to normal and start the repair process. It took time for the cells to be circulated and as he follows the instructions, slowly, but surely, Dad was able to regain strength and endurance. The reality of him getting better and getting closer to coming home for the holidays was actually coming true. His eyes start to light up and his cheeks perk up more. The whole time he was in the hospital, he remained hopeful about his recovery and still encouraged everyone who came to see him. And I mean EVERYONE came to see him! Our Pastor, our church family, our extended family, his co-workers, his friends, EVERYONE! He's in the hospital fighting for his life and yet still has time to pray for everyone that visited him and kept them laughing through their struggles. We were glad he encouraged so many people, but we were ready for him to come home. Like, ok God this isn't cute anymore. Let's wrap this saga up and get home. And when I say wrap it up, I mean no more diminishing health and full life (I must be specific with God).

Sometimes the Lord lets you live with a thorn in your flesh, because you CAN live with a thorn in your flesh.

The righteous person may have many troubles, but the Lord delivers him from them all.

-Psalms 34:19 NIV

Chapter 4: The Getaway

Dad finally was able to come home just in time for Christmas and we were relieved! That's all we kept praying for that we would all be able to celebrate Christmas at home. That was the best Christmas gift our family could ever receive and experience. We were able to eat dinner at the table and continue with our normal traditions without being interrupted by hospital staff or doctors. Dad was glad to be home in his normal element and spend time with family and not worry about preparing for the next process of the procedure or taking the next round of medications. Of course, Dad was on some new medication and one of them, the steroids, started to kick in. It threw his appetite overboard. Sweets were his weakness. He loved pecan pies, cakes, cookies, candy bars, and chocolate clusters. Snacks like chips, Fiddle Faddle (or you young folks call it Crunch n' Munch), and honey buns would vanish from the kitchen before anyone would notice they were there. Food commercials killed him. As soon as a Burger King commercial came on, he was hungry and wanted that burger NOW. Any food commercial he saw, it was snack time. They showed those things every 30 seconds, and he would say "Ah come on!! They have to advertise every piece of food RIGHT NOW?!" He definitely didn't miss ANY meals. His weight went from 160lbs to 210lbs for what seemed to be overnight. Because of the stem cell therapy lowering his immune system, he had to have fresh food properly cooked so he couldn't eat leftovers; only fresh food every day. Thismeant we either had to cook or eat out every day! Just bourgeois!

Mom and I are eating hot dogs while he's having medium well steaks!

While he's recuperating at home, the doctors keep in contact with us and informed us of a few changes. Our family knew there would be a difference in his normal day, but we took them in stride and learned to adjust. One of the things we had to adjust to was "the smell". There's a process during stem cell therapy when doctors take your blood cells out and harvest them until it's time to transfer them back into the body. They put them in this cold, gooey solution to keep the blood cells preserved for a certain amount of time. Apparently, the solution has organic ingredients in it and when it all mixes together, it smells like garlic. Yeah, garlic. That isn't so bad, but keep in mind that the blood cells have been marinating in this garlic smelling solution for about a month. So, guess what? It makes you smell like garlic from the inside out. Dad smelled like garlic every hour of every day. He couldn't do anything about it because it's internal. He couldn't wash it off, couldn't bathe in tomato sauce or oatmeal to get it off, and he couldn't just mask it with body lotion. He literally gave off a naturally garlic smelling aroma. And get this! He couldn't smell himself at all. Like how do you NOT smell garlic coming from your own skin? But it's one of the things the doctors warned us about. Dad couldn't smell the garlic, but the rest of us can. It. Filled. The. Room. Quickly! He was self-conscious about it, and we didn't want him to feel bad, but he had a garlicky aroma. One day, Dad asked a church member who was also in the Brotherhood Choir with him if he could pick me up from school. His friend was happy to help and agreed to pick me up. Dad decided to ride with him just to get out of the house and feel the fresh air for a change. They're riding in his truck and once I noticed it, I hop in and enjoy the short ride. They're in the front seat having a conversation as normal when mid conversation Dad interrupts and says to his friend,

"Hey, I forgot to mention that you know I had that stem cell transfer done and it's got a side effect."

"Ha, don't they all."

Dad tries to him "but this one smells like garlic because of the solution they put back in me."

"Oh ok"

"So, it makes me smell like garlic. I mean I bathe every day; I don't want anyone thinking I'm out here just not clean……. Do you smell anything like garlic?"

"Nah, you're ok."

Me, on the other hand, I'm quietly saying "yes dad, YOU DO."

"Oh, ok. Just checking cause unfortunately, I can't get rid of it. I just have to wait until it plays out."

His friend reassures him by saying, "You're ok."

They continued their original conversation until we made it home. While they were talking, I kept wondering why Dad felt the need to apologize for his condition. If this life saving procedure ends up making you smell like garlic, then smell like garlic! At least you're alive to smell like garlic. Rather it be garlic than three-day old musk! Do I like that he smells like garlic, NO! But I'm glad he's at home with me filling up the whole house with his aroma.

But when it finally wore off, Mom and I were glad! Mom waited until the smell started wearing off before she complained about it out loud. She was getting sick of it. Thank God for healing and thankGod it wore off.

Now the road to recovery continues…. again.

Over the next couple of years, my parents will get to be parents instead of full-time cancer patients and they are definitely parenting. Now that I want to hang out with friends and get out of the house some, they do this thing where they like to know where I'm going. In my opinion, you're going to know where I'm going because you'll be dropping me off. I ask to go to the usual places like the mall, the movies, a friend's party, or to the park. I had my group of friends and my best friend around me that kept me motivated, focused, and full of laughter. Bestie and I were always trying to figure out a way to get out of the house. The normal "if you ask then my mom will say yes" or "if you go, she'll let me go too" kind of shenanigans. All this planning and we didn't have any money or any ride to do the things we wanted to do. I hated asking my parents for money just so I could go out because I knew we didn't have it. Going from a two-income household down to one income while the other parent recovered then back to two incomes was a financial strain. Every time Mom would ask what I was going to eat while I was out, I would just tell her that I would eat before leaving the house. She would say "Child you can't go anywhere without any money! Go bring me my purse." She would always give me a $10 or $20 bill and I would spend every bit of it. Sometimes I would save my lunch money up for the weekends. Instead of eating lunch, I would pocket that money and just eat a Payday candy bar. I did what I could to not miss out on any fun. Where Bestie went, I went, and we had the best fun. If we kept our grades up and our attitudes right, our parents would let us go out and have fun. Bestie and I are still hanging tough until this day living our lives out loud and fulfilling our dreams.

Graduation is coming upon us, and I feel like I'm going to miss my high school friends. The homecoming games, proms, band practices, football games, and summer parties will forever leave me with epic memories. Even though some people thought I was stuck up or weird, I really didn't care. I was just glad this household was healthy again and I could enjoy my senior year of high school with laughter and future aspirations. Though I should've got better grades and a higher score on the ACT as my dad told me numerous times, I still did well as a B average student. During my senior year, students decided to plan a senior trip to Panama City Beach, Florida during Spring Break. Yep! The epic Spring Break shenanigans. We would enjoy the beach, go to the famous Tiki Bar, and ride up and down the strip like we were grown. I told my parents about it as if it was the greatest idea ever. They quickly looked at me as if I were crazy. I had no concrete answer to their questions: Where are you all going to stay? Who all is going? Who is that? Who are their parents? Are their parents going? Who's driving? How much does it cost? I'm thinking "Lord, ALL THESE QUESTIONS!!" Clearly, they were in parenting mode. I kept reminding them daily about the trip. As time got closer to go on the trip, more and more students backed out for various reasons. My parents kept listening to me explain why I should go with my main case being "this is my chance to show you that I'm responsible on my own away from home." Finally, we were able to come to a resolution.

Mom gave me her final blessing with "fine, we'll let you go, but you need to find out the names of whose going and get their parents' contact information. You'll need to call us every day and let us know where you are."

"Wait now. I didn't think we were letting her go. By herself?" Dad said in confusion.

"She's not going by herself; she's going with her class."

"I don't think she should go. She hasn't traveled without us before."

"We have to let her go at some point. Might as well start now. She'll be going off to college soon, so we need to get used to it. She's going to leave anyway."

"We can wait until that time" Dad said firmly.

"I will call every day and let you know when we get there. I'll keep my phone on," is what I told them to reassure them that I was responsible.

Dad reluctantly replies with "…. you know it's some crazies out there. Don't be out all night, just go on back inside."

"I'll be safe."

Like normal, over 30 students signed up to go, but only five went. Myself and three of my friends plus two young adults to keep an eye on us. The six of us loaded up the car and for some odd reason I have to sit in the middle of the front seat like some child. What does me being small have to do with having to sit in the middle? What am I, TWELVE?! Ugh!

We went down to Florida for almost a week with what seemed like $800 between all of us. After a six-hour drive, we were ready to get out of the car and enjoy the sun. We ate cheap food, met interesting people who were also on spring break, and stayed out all day finding things to get into. It was the most fun and exciting week! On the night before we left, we decided to wind down and pack up our stuff and ended up leaving the beach that night a little early to head back to the hotel. We were waiting in a little bit of traffic to get off the beach, but we weren't worried about it since there was no rush to get back. All week we had the music blasting in the car with the windows down, but that night we barely had the radio turned up. We were kind of tired from the week, so we just sat in the car quietly. It was a quiet night ride home with just a gentle breeze in the air.

BOOM!!

A drunk driver slammed into the back of the car which made us slam into the SUV in front of us. Yes, I was sitting in the middle seat up front, so my knees hit the front panel. We were shaken up, but ok. A little whiplash and knee pain were the only damages we incurred physically. We kept saying to each other "where did he come from? We were the last car in traffic. He didn't even slam on his brakes." The drunk driver could barely exit his car and check on us without falling to the ground. He was a basket case! Our car was damaged in the back and the front and looked completely inoperable. We just stood back and looked at the car wondering how we were going to get home. That night all of us were wondering how we were going to tell our parents that we were in a car accident six hours away from home. After talking with the police officers to file a report and checking that we were all physically ok, we get back into the banged-up car and slowly head back to our hotel. There we were, four out of six of us, trying to conjure up whether to tell our parents or not. Finally, we decide to tell them….in the morning…… when we get back. We convinced ourselves that if we told them right then, they would never let us go out of town again. We all tossed and turned that night and barely slept until it was time to go. We loaded back into the car and hoped that we would make it back safely. The car moved slowly so instead of it taking six hours to get back, it took almost eight hours. We are struggling to do even the minimum speed on the highway, but the Lord kept pushing our car along. We finally made it back home that night and I called my parents to let them know we made it back safely. My friend's mother drops me back off at home and my parents welcome me in with open arms. They asked me how the trip went and all the fun things we did. They were glad to see me back home safe and sound. Mom noticed that I was moving around weirdly and asked what was wrong. I simply replied "Nah, my neck just hurts a little. I must have slept wrong." There was no reason for me NOT to tell them about the accident and yet I kept it a secret. My right knee and my neck kept hurting for the next couple of days, but I managed to get through the pain. Mom kept noticing something was off but didn't dig deeper into it. Until there was a phone call. My friend's mother called to give all the parents an update on the accident. She told my mom that the drunk driver was at fault and will be replacing the car. They have a lengthy phone call and I walk in on the conversation right when my mom says "So that's why Monica has been acting weird. The girl's been in an accident!! She didn't tell me anything about it!" Of course, she fussed at me for not telling them about it. Mom said they wouldn't have been mad, but just wanted to make sure I was ok. The typical questions were "why didn't you say anything? When did it happen? HOW did the car make it back? Who was driving? Who else was hurt?" were quickly asked and this time I had all the answers. Mom firmly said the Lord was with us during this trip. They were concerned about me like normal parents. It was just different this time because I'm usually concerned about them. I guess I didn't tell them about the accident because I didn't want them to worry about it with all the other stuff going on. Or maybe I thought I could handle it on my own. Or maybe I thought it was just a little accident compared to all the other things going on. Regardless, I should've told them.

I was nervous about life after high school, but also ready to see what it had in store. I had been so caught up in what was going on in our household that I barely focused on what was going on in the world. I was so consumed with my parents that I didn't realize how quickly I would be off on my own. I started thinking more about how I was going to achieve my goals and how I was going to stay on pace. I wanted to make myself proud more than I wanted to make my parents proud of me. I needed to prove to myself how I can turn my actions into results and be self-sufficient. I had things to think about leading up to graduation. I knew that my next phase of life would be the foundation of a new beginning.

Congrats to the graduating class of 2004! Off to college I go!

My son, do not forget my teaching, but keep my commands in your heart, for they will prolong your life many years and bring you peace and prosperity.

-Proverbs 3: 1-2 NIV

Chapter 5: I'm leaving!

Now that I've graduated, I need to make some money before heading off to college. Mom is off during the summers since teachers get a summer break unless they decide to teach summer school. While she's off, Mom takes on a part time job to make some extra money before the next school year starts. Since I have some extra time and just turned 18 right after graduation, she suggested that I come to work with her so I can make my own money. I agreed and I went with her to apply for a warehouse job that would start in the next few days. I put my application in and prepared for my first day of work at my first job. Mom briefed me on the schedule and the different things they'd have us do during the shift. The job was at a warehouse just a few miles from where we lived where they packaged goods, such as electronics, DVDs, DVD players, etc., and prepared to ship them out to stores. We both signed up for the early morning shift and I mean it's EARLY. We had to BE THERE at seven in the morning! That means I had to wake up at five in the morning just to get ready and make the 20-minute drive. Mom and I got up to shower and made our lunches before heading out. She made us ham and cheese sandwiches while I grabbed a bag of chips and fruit to put in our lunch bags. She told me we would only get a 30-minute lunch, so we won't have time to leave the campus to pick something up. I was fine with that, and it didn't bother me at all. I was just curious about how the workday was going to be. We hopped in the car and made our way to the warehouse to clock-in for the workday. It's a whole line of people walking in to work so it takes a little time for them to tell us where we'll be stationed. Finally, I'm told where I'll be packaging

DVDs for the day in the warehouse. The managers told me about bathroom breaks, my lunch break, and where to clock out at the end of the day. Mom snuck up behind them to tell me "If you need to take a break just go to the bathroom cause these folks don't care about these work conditions. You'll be standing up all day in this hot room for a whole 8-hour shift. They don't care! So just take a break when you need to cause when I feel tired, I just go hide in the bathroom for 20 minutes." I walked over to my workstation and started learning what to do. I'm working with three other ladies, and they teach me the process. It's simple: flip, inspect, pack. Flip each double-DVD pack over to make sure it's sealed. Inspect the back to make sure the barcode is visible in the bottom right corner. Pack it into the box so that the next person can start sealing the box up. Easy. The DVDs came down a long conveyor belt fast enough to pack items in a short amount of time, but slow enough to prevent it from being hectic. Each person stood about six feet from each other along the conveyor belt where we would end up packing thousands of boxes. It's productive easy work that I thought was ok doing. I could do this daily.

It's about 9am now and I start feeling lightheaded. It happens suddenly, but I brush it off. It starts getting worse to where I have to squat down for a minute. The girl next to me asked if I'm ok and I reassured her I'm fine and pretended that I was squatting down to tie my shoe. I stood back up and felt a little better. I continued working and tried to have a conversation, but my words just weren't coming out right. Clearly there's something off so I told my co-worker that I'm going to the bathroom. The bathroom was only a few steps away across the warehouse, but it seemed like it took me forever to get there.

I wobbled to the bathroom and sat down on the toilet seat. The Lord knows I never sit down on a public toilet seat or barely even use one for that matter, but this situation called for a different behavior. I sat there for a few minutes to get myself together and tried to figure out why I'm feeling this way. After five minutes, I got up, washed my hands, and headed back to the floor. As I'm walking back, I see my mother heading to the bathroom too. As she walked past me, she said, "time for my break!" and we both laughed. I got back to my station to finish working and the lightheadedness and nausea came up on me fast. One minute I'm working then the next minute…….

……. I'm waking up. WAKING UP!?! When did I go to sleep? Why is everyone in my face and HOW did I end up on the floor? This floor is dirty, why am I down here? What is happening?

Everyone was asking me "are you ok?" while I had this confused look on my face. Then they said in unison, "she's waking up."

All I could think was "she who?" They then asked, "can you talk?" which I thought was a stupid question to ask. I've been talking all my life. I try to get up off the floor when one of the co-workers says, "take it easy getting up. Go slow." I'm wondering why he's telling me to go slow and I end up motioning my hand to everyone to back up. I could hear another co-worker in the background saying, "she was just talking to me, but she wasn't making any sense then I turn around and she's on the floor. She was fine just a minute ago."

"Wait, what happened?" I yelled.

"You passed out."

"When?" (and where was I)

I'm finally able to sit up, but everyone is still crowded around me, which kept frustrating me. Like back up! We're in this huge warehouse and I still can't breathe with everyone around me. I'm still trying to understand what happened. I've never passed out before, so this is new to me, and my head hurts so bad. I tried to stand up, but everyone said, "waitfor the ambulance." AMBULANCE! What. Is. Going. On!

A man finally noticed that I looked confused and asked me "you don't know what's going on, do you?" I told him no and he explained what happened as a paramedic was walking up behind him. He said "you passed out at your station and when you began to fall, you fell to your knees first then your head hit the metal bar under the conveyor table. You've been out ever since until now." After he explained that to me, I felt some liquid come down the right side of my face and low and behold; it's blood. The paramedics looked me over, asked me how I felt, and about any medications. They brought me a wheelchair and talked to my mom about what happened. They told her to take me straight to the hospital since I was ok enough to not have to ride in the ambulance. They rolled me out to the car and sent me off. While driving to the hospital, Mom asked me what happened. I told her I wasn't sure, but I felt lightheaded first and then woke up onthe floor.

We got to the hospital and waited in the emergency room to be seen. Again, my sister's authority gets me back to see a doctor sooner rather than later. She OWNS that hospital (at least to me she does). I'm sitting in my patient room with

Mom and my head is still killing me. The nurse comes in and asked me how I'm feeling and if I needed anything. I told her I'm fine besides my head hurting and I asked the nurse if I could have some painkillers. She tells me "No, you can't have any pain medication right now. I can give you ice chips though."

"Ice chips? What's that supposed to do?"

"It helps to give you some relief and get your mind off the pain for a little while."

"But my head hurts."

"I know, but if we give you pain medicine the doctor won't know if the side effects are from the medicine or your head injury. He needs to evaluate all your symptoms to figure out if any damage was done before giving you medicine. Until then, you can have ice chips."

"Ok...may I have a snack."

The nurse laughed and said "No, you can't have a snack yet. I'll bring you some ice chips and a Sprite."

So, I must sit here in pain for no one knows the day nor the hour of when I'll be to see the doctor. I'm in pain, hungry, uncomfortable, and bothered and all I can get right now is a cup of Sprite on ice. I lay there in the hospital bed and endured the pain. This is when I realized my pain tolerance is high and my patience is long. Mom is talking to Dad on the phone about what happened and about how long we'll be in the hospital. This is different because it's usually me at the other end of the room checking up on my parents. I continue watching cartoons with my little cup of ICE CHIPS.

The doctor finally comes in and does his normal introduction. He asked Mom and I about what happened and if I had experienced this before. The doctor ordered some tests while feeling around my head for anything out of the ordinary. I have a cut on the right side of my head close to my temple and he insisted on running some tests to see what's going on. What I thought would be a quick trip to the ER turned out to be an ordeal of lengthy tests and assessments. I would rather be safe than sorry though. Mom on the other hand, is worried. She kept asking the doctors what led to me passing out and they haven't found the answers yet. Throughout all this, I'm still wondering about that pain medicine they keep promising me and some food.

The doctors ran several tests, and it turns out I have a hairline fracture in my skull on my right side right above my temple. I have a what?! How hard did I fall? How big was that metal bar? I didn't even bleed enough to have a fracture. After telling me the results and discussing some scenarios with my family, the doctors decided that surgery isn't necessary since it's not pressing against my brain and the fracture is hidden underneath my hair. They will keep me in the hospital for a couple of days to watch me for any new side effects. The doctor stated that I'm lucky that it wasn't worse but assures me that I'll be fine. And yes, now I can take pain medicine. I eat, take some pain medicine and then fall fast asleep as it had been a long, eventful day.

By this time, it's nighttime and sister is off her nursing shift. She comes up to my room, which is now on the neurological floor of the hospital to check on me and see how our parents are holding up. I'm the baby of the house so now I'm being babied. My family doesn't think I should go away to college but instead stay closer to home due to this incident. Apparently, this head injury will live with me a long time instead of it being just a quick mishap like I thought. The doctors could not figure out why I passed out because everything went back to normal and there was nothing out of the ordinary. Seems like I passed out randomly with no sign of an illness or my health being compromised. Mom, Dad and sister are discussing what's best for me while I'm lying in the hospital bed listening to their discussion. How are they deciding what will work for me without considering what I want to do? I know they're older and have better insight, but what about what I want to do? I know this head injury isn't the end because there has to be more to life than this. It didn't turn me stupid; it just made a little dent in my head. So, I fell and bumped my head, no biggie! The wheels still turn the same. Maybe I'm not taking it as seriously as I should be, but it's not that big of a deal breaker to me.

After a couple of days in the hospital, I'm finally able to go home. All my follow up tests came back fine and there have been no unusual side effects happening so now I'm free to go. I'm ready to be home because the nurses coming in every other hour to check on me is really getting old. I thank God it wasn't worse, but I'm glad for this experience because I know how my parents feel when they're in the hospital and have to deal with restrictions. This experience also helped me to know who God is to me. I hear testimonies from people at church and I sing the hymns, but that's God from someone else's perspective. This injury is helping me learn who God is to me, for me, with me. I don't know why I passed out, but I know God was there and is still here with me throughout this experience. Am I supposed to know why

I went through this. I'm not sure, but my eyes are open now. I see you God; I see you in the background. Now I'm heading back home and getting back to normal. I guess there is no job for me right now.

I didn't want to stay home in Huntsville for college. Nothing wrong with staying home, but I felt too sheltered and too close to home. I wanted to get away for a while. I figured that since my parents were better and regaining their physical strength that I could go away and start the second part of my life. I felt it was time to leave to live my own life and figure out how to get to law school. My goal was to attend college, then head to law school, and eventually be an attorney with the Securities and Exchange Commission (SEC). I wanted to tackle those individuals and corporations who were stealing funds through stock trading. To start my career journey, I REALLY wanted to attend Southern University in Baton Rouge, Louisiana. Even though I've never been to Louisiana or to Southern University's campus, I fell in love with their band and their majorettes and wanted to continue being a majorette there. I wanted to learn the culture there and be surrounded by other Black students matriculating in black greatness that disputes corporate environments, in a good way. So, I applied well before high school graduation. My parents knew I had an interest in going there, but they would rather me stay home though. They even tried to bribe me.

"We'll buy you a car if you go to Alabama A&M University" Mom suggested. I knew they couldn't afford it, but I still entertained the conversation. I told her, "Nope, I want to go to Southern." I low-key thought, these people are not going to buy me a car. My parents then asked, "What can we do to make you stay here?"

"Let me go to Southern."

So, I sent the application off.

And waited.

And waited.

AND WAITED!

High school graduation came and went. And no letter from Southern University. So, my backup plan was to apply to Stillman College. I knew nothing about the school other than it was an HBCU and it was away from home but close enough to make a quick trip. I applied just to say I had a backup school in mind. I did a short, nonchalant prayer about it, but nothing like the prayer I had for Southern, and left it alone. I was just mad and disappointed that I hadn't heard from Southern yet. It was worse than getting rejected by a boy, like really? A WHOLE SCHOOL doesn't want me?! Ugh!

It only took Stillman two weeks to respond to my application and accept me as a new student. Good news: I got accepted!! Bad news: I got accepted. Now my prayer was,

"Lord, I got accepted into Stillman, but is that where I should really be going? Do I continue to wait for Southern? Would Stillman set me up for success? Time is running out for me you know. When are you going to sit next to me and tell me what to do?"

Even though I prayed, I didn't take time out to listen to God's response. I just kept moving along with what I thought was the plan. Time continued to pass as I waited and the closer it gets to the start of a new semester, the more anxious I become about selecting my school. A few weeks have passed and now it's move-in week for college freshmen at Stillman. I reluctantly started thinking about what to pack and started realizing that I'm going to Stillman whether I like it or not. My parents were pleased with Stillman since it's only a two-hour drive away from home compared to a six-hour drive to Southern University. Plus, there's no out-of-state fees. I don't tell them how deeply disappointed I am about not attending Southern, but I accepted it for what it is and kept moving forward.

While I'm stuffing my suitcases to head two hours away to Stillman, a letter came in the mail for me. Yep, it's Southern with my acceptance letter. WHY ARE YOU JUST NOW LETTING ME KNOW?

"Lord, you funny! You are on time with these jokes too, I see. We can't afford a last-minute trip to fly to Louisiana or take that long drive to get there with all this stuff. I don't even have a scholarship for them. Fine! I'll just go to Stillman and make the best of it. And help me close this suitcase!!"

The family and I loaded up in my sister's SUV early the next morning to drive two hours south to Stillman College. My suitcases full of shoes, clothes, and accessories are jam packed and fill up the trunk quickly. As we were making the drive, I realized that today will be my first day on the campus and experiencing college life. During the ride, we talked about old memories, my parents' college experiences and what not to do on campus.

Whenever we go on road trips, Mom always has to stop and eat mainly because she's diabetic and has to take her medicine at a certain time. But also, she just likes to stop and eat. Now on the other hand, sister is always the driver on road trips and likes to just get to the destination. Since we're on a schedule to make it to campus by a certain time to go through admissions and check-in, we all decide to just eat when we get to the campus, except for Mom. She wants to eat before we get there.

"Um I need to stop and get something to eat" she says from the back seat.

My sister responded with, "Yeah we'll stop when we get to Tuscaloosa."

"No. I need to eat before then because I need to take my medicine. I'm diabetic so I need to eat on a schedule."

"Two hours won't kill you. We have to get Monica down to Stillman by a certain time."

"It won't take that long for us to stop and get something to eat. It's just the drive thru. Or let me out and I'll go in and get it."

"You can wait" my sister says as she continues to drive down the highway. My mother's anger continued to grow, and I was just sitting in the back seat wondering what kind of friends I'll make in college.

We finally make it to Stillman and go through the admissions process that seemed to take forever. This is when I learned how expensive college *really* is. It's like millions of dollars!! So, I'll be doing some work study to help pay for tuition. We find out which residence hall I'll be in then Mom says, "I'll be back." I assume she's going to the bathroom and pay it no mind. The admission department handed me my class schedule and let me know where I can buy my books, then Dad pays for my tuition, room and board, and dining account. Dad and I walked over to my residence hall to find out which room I'll be in and my roommate. He asked me,

"Where's your mother?"

"I don't know, she said she'll be back."

"Maybe she's with your sister."

My sister and niece unloaded the car with all my stuff, and they helped me get moved into my dorm room at Roulhac Hall.

"Where's Mom?" asked my sister.

Dad response by telling her "We thought she caught up with you."

"Where did she go? She doesn't have any keys and doesn't know anyone here."

Meanwhile, I find out I'm on the second floor so taking things upstairs becomes interesting since the residence hall only has one elevator for the three-story building. We take turns getting things up and down the stairs and learn about the girls that will be staying in the hall. It seems like it takes forever to get all my stuff up to the second floor and unpack. We sanitize my small bathroom and the shared refrigerator in the middle. Sister starts to suggest different ways to decorate my room.

"You should get some organizers for your desk to make extra space."

"I've tried calling your mother, but she still hasn't answered the phone" said Dad as he eagerly tries to figure out where Mom is while we're talking about decorations.

"What color do you want your room to be?" sister asks me.

"I'm thinking purple like a purple comforter with gray sheets. Maybe curtains."

"I going to go look for your mother" as Dad tells us while leaving my dorm room.

"She couldn't have gone far" my sister tells him before the door closes.

I'm still thinking about decorating and organizing and I suggest "Maybe some storage containers too."

"Yeah, you'll need those."

Dad tells us "I'll be back" as he pops his head in from the hallway after taking a quick look for Mom.

"OK" sister and I responded in unison.

We cleaned my side of the dorm room, organized my clothes and shoes, and were ready to go shopping for my bedding. We left the residence hall and headed to the parkinglot to go shopping. We FINALLY saw Mom.

"Where have you been?" sister yells at her.

With a surprised look on her face as if she didn't know we were looking for her, Mom says "Out getting something to eat."

"With who??" we both say in confusion.

"I met this nice lady down by the admission's office and I was telling her that I needed to eat something and how my family wouldn't stop and get me something to eat...."

"Really" is the only thing sister could say out of frustration.

"....so, she took me to get something to eat."

"...with a complete stranger."

"Yeah, she was really nice."

Dad then walks up behind Mom and yells "Where have youbeen?! We've been looking for you!"

Sometimes parents are so grown that they don't follow directions and run off and do their own thing. After figuring out where Mom had gone for two hours, we hopped in the car and headed to the nearest home goods store to get towels, bedding, storage bins, and extra pillows for my room. It's nice to see everyone bringing in their ideas on how to decorate and organize my room. It's a good family moment. This is also the start of a stronger relationship with my sister since now we have something in common. I'm trying to catch up with her and her life.

We headed back to my dorm room and finished decorating with my new stuff. We all worked together to make my room as cozy and functional as possible with the little space I have.

It finally all comes together. And now it's time for my family to say goodbye.

Sister goes first and says "Bye! Call if you need anything, you'll have fun here." Unfortunately, my niece has started crying and I mean it's an ugly cry. Dad tells me "We're proud of you. We'll miss you. Let us know if you need anything and watch out for the crazies. Just give us a call."

Mom on the other hand is in her feelings and in her distress, she says, "MY BABY!" Mind you, my niece is still in tears. I tell them all that "I'll miss you all. I'll call if I need anything. I'll let you know how everything goes. I love you all."

Yes, my niece is STILL crying and can only bury her head in my shoulder.

We shared tight hugs and "I love you" between each other. It's time for me to set my mark and follow my career dreams while matriculating at Stillman. I knew my career pathway, where I wanted to be and how to get there. Just had to follow the steps.

In their hearts humans plan their course, but the Lord establishes their steps.

-Proverbs 16:9 NIV

Chapter 6: Well, This is New!

PREGNANT?!!

Really, Monica?

My second year of college and I got pregnant. I felt as if I disappointed myself. How was I going to navigate this? How am I supposed to be a mother? Why did I let this happen? I felt like I messed up my plans. Delayed or maybe ruined my goals. How could I finally leave the house and get a chance to do it for myself only to get pregnant? I'm still learning to care for myself and now I must figure out how to care for a baby. Is this who I am? Someone that will always be caring for someone else? Am I the kind of person that must feel needed in order to feel fulfilled? So many thoughts and so little time.

The Bible teaches us how and why we should forgive others, but it was hard trying to forgive myself. It's easy to ask for forgiveness, but it's hard to have mercy when I'm too critical of myself. There were times I told myself,

"Monica, you messed up. You had a plan and YOU messed it up. Get it together!!"

My mother insisted that I come back home and finish school there. I disagreed and said I would finish my last two years at Stillman and have my baby with me. She said,

"You're not going back down there. You're going to stay here."

"But my credits are at Stillman. My class schedule is already done. They gave me a laptop. I got to move back in."

"You'll get your credits transferred. You're not going back. No, you will take care of your responsibilities here back home where you'll have some help and stay focused."

I was so mad! I didn't want to transfer my credits and change schools in the middle of my college years. In my mind, I would get a part time job and find a daycare for my son all while taking classes during the day. I would find an apartment close to campus to make it easier to get back and forth to class, even though I didn't have a car. I had this whole plan in my head even though it wasn't solid. It didn't make sense, but it was my plan. Mom shut all that down and had me move everything back home and start the process of transferring my credits. I complained about the whole process of transferring my credits. Of course, I wanted to continue going to an HBCU, so I researched how to transfer all my credits from Stillman to Alabama A&M University. I had well over 30 credit hours to transfer heading into my junior year of college. I was thinking transferring credit hours from one HBCU to another HBCU would be easy. No, no it was not. Because of differences in school curriculum and the level of difficulty related to educational coursework, Alabama A&M would only accept 16 credit hours from Stillman. WHAT?! Why only accept 16 of my credits based on class description and coursework not matching up? That's ridiculous! I'll basically be starting over. I decided that since all my credits could not transfer that it was another reason to stay at Stillman. See, my plan will work out anyway. Mom said, "Let's try UAH." Excuse me. UAH as in the University of Alabama-Huntsville. A PWI. Me at a PWI? Why?

I go to UAH just to entertain her idea and say I did it. The admissions counselor and the Dean of Liberal Arts reviewed my transcript and my course levels. Low and behold they agreed to accept 24 of my 34 credits. Transferring my credits from Stillman to UAH would mean I would keep my status as an incoming junior, only lose credits in my general studies classes, and maintain my GPA. So, Lord, you want ME to transfer from an HBCU to a PWI and be ok with it? I'm the same little girl that told my mom at eight years old to take me out of one elementary school and transfer me to another elementary school because I was the only black girl there. At that time, I wanted students to be the same color as me. And now 12 years later, I'm having to transfer to a PWI. Lord, you funny! Reluctantly, I completed the transfer student application, got my financial aid to cover my tuition at UAH, and prepared to start my junior year in the fall. Even though things were falling into place, I didn't like it because it wasn't coming together like I wanted it to. I didn't want to transfer schools, I didn't want to go to a PWI, and I didn't want to be back in my parent's house again. I was so mad and frustrated that I didn't ask God why this was happening to me. I asked him what am I supposed to learn from this situation because there has to be an upside to what I considered to be foolishness. You mean to tell me having a baby is going to flip my whole world upside down?!

EXHALE

From this point on in my life, whenever I'm going through something I stopped asking "Why Lord?" and I only ask, "What do I need to learn from this?"

The summer heading into my junior year of college, my son was born. On June 8th I had the sweetest and quietest little baby. The most handsome full-headed boy that was ever made in the world! He's precious. I wasn't ready to be a mother and definitely not ready to take care of someone again, but here he is. Once I became a mother, I instantly became territorial and protective of my son. Even on the day he was born, the nurses tried to take him to the nursery so I could get a little rest.

"Let's take him down to the nursery so you can sleep and get some rest" the nurse suggested, but I wasn't having it. I firmly told her, "No, he will stay here with me."

"But this is your last chance to rest because it will change after this."

"Then I will get used to the change now. He's staying with me."

Dad stayed in the hospital room with me my first night as a new mother. He slept in the uncomfortable hospital chair in the room and would wake up every time my son would cry just to make sure I was ok. He slept when I slept and was awake when I woke up. Mom would then come by the next morning and bring my clothes, blankets, snacks and extra pajamas. My parents would take turns looking after my son and I until it was time to go home from the hospital. Once my son was home, I knew that from here on out, my decisions would affect his future. I knew being a young mother was not my goal, but it was time to make the best of it. I had to provide a life where my son could thrive in greatness regardless of how he got here. I prayed,

Lord, you obviously let me have this child because you have a plan for him. I don't know how to raise a child so since you gave him to me, I'm giving him back to you. You tell me what to do and how to raise him for your will because I don't know what I'm doing, but I know that YOU know the plans for him. So here! You raise him.

After that prayer, I felt better about being a mother and came to accept the need for me to transfer schools. Mom was right. I would need help raising my son. My parents were supportive of my son and I and made sure that we had all of life's necessities. They never made me feel like a burden, but I felt like I was one from time to time. They were just being parents to their child that just had a baby.

The end of summer was approaching and the fall semester at UAH was starting. Switching from an HBCU to a PWI was a huge culture shock. I went from living on campus two hours away from home to living off campus in my parent's home, so college life was a huge shift. Plus, I have a history of disliking attending all white schools. I felt lost, unseen, and disconnected from everyone and everything. Everyone already had their friend groups, and I was just THERE. UAH is a good school, very commendable, but just wasn't for me. I lost my focus, my motivation, and myself. Switching schools was horrible. Totally would not recommend…. zero stars. But I had to make the best of it since I have a son at home now. I quickly learned that it wasn't about me not liking the school, but it's about setting a foundation for a better life for me and my son and that started with finishing my degree. UAH was not easy, but definitely worth it. My sister graduated from UAH, so this gave me another reason to be like her.

So, from then on, I dedicated myself to raising my son the best way I knew how, while still trying to forgive myself. I was still learning about myself, my purpose, and what I'm supposed to do with the talents that I have. I knew having a son was not the end of my journey but would later realize it was the beginning of a path full of love and sacrifice. Would I still go to law school? Would I be a good attorney like my role model Jocelyn Jones Boustani? Can I raise a child of good character? How will I change in the next 10 years? These questions would stay with me a long time, but I knew being a single mother was not my title nor my ending. There's got to be more to life than my limitations.

I wouldn't change anything about my life at this moment besides the fact I should've traveled more.

Be kind and compassionate to one another, forgiving each other, just as in Christ God forgave you.

– Ephesians 4:32 NIV

Chapter 7: What Now??

Whew! Raising a kid is NOT for the weak!

Raising a child, especially a Black son, is a blessed roller coaster of emotions, activities, and troubles. My son and I have fun together and I enjoy seeing him grow into his personality more. I take him with me everywhere I go so he gets to experience the world in different environments like birthday parties, banquets, stage plays, aquariums, and every church event known to man. I could tell my son is very intuitive and not friendly. He observes first, then decides if he likes someone or something later. He's like a younger version of me and it's quite interesting watching him grow up. It's like watching me grow up but in another person.

He's in pre-school now and enjoying his little friends. This timeframe is full of fields trips, midterm tests, work schedules, children's events, and homework. My dad helps to pick up the slack when I'm not around my son due to class or work schedule. He plays with my son, teaches him life tricks, takes him outside to play, and makes the usual store run to pick up his favorite snacks. They're getting along just fine like two friends just hanging out.

Then Dad has a regular appointment. Completely routine, only this time the doctor's discovered prostate cancer.

Prostate cancer! Cancer just loves hanging out with our family and it's really annoying. At this time, I'm really irritated with sickness, especially with it coming back-to-back. With this news, I cried for like 2 minutes straight. I rarely cry unless It's because I'm laughing too hard so I can count on both hands exactly how many times I've cried when it's not associated with laughter. I cried not because I was sad, but I'm mad that my dad is going through this again. Like dang, leave the man alone!! Ain't he been through enough!! He's not Job; we already have that story. We don't need two! The Lord knows Mom can't handle it! And why does he have to have ALL the cancers? We didn't ask for the variety pack of cancer, and we barely asked for the free trial!

Dad goes in for the consultation, again, on how the procedure will be conducted to treat prostate cancer and the side effects after. Since it's prostate cancer, I don't ask many questions. I felt THAT business was not my business. Plus, I was a bit distracted during this time because I was busy raising my son. I kept thinking that I missed noticing any new symptoms or changes in behavior and how this diagnosis was a bit of a shock to me. I usually notice changes in my parents' health but missed this sickness coming along. After the consultation and some weeks at home to decide the next steps, Dad goes to the hospital to have the procedure and then comes home to recuperate. It slows him down for a little while then he's eventually back to normal. No red devil this time.

I started questioning my own health because after seeing my parents go through so much sickness, I needed to be more conscious of my eating habits and physical well-being. I must watch my own symptoms and illnesses and make sure I'm noticing changes in my body. I rarely get sick besides the occasional cold and laryngitis. Every now and then, I get my blood pressure, blood sugar, and heart rate checked along with my mammograms just to make sure everything is working well. I've got to stay healthy for myself, my son, and clearly for my parents because they are just sickly.

Dad started getting back to his normal energy levels and his eating habits. We're glad that he's packing on weight and staying at a healthy 200 lbs. since we've already experienced his lowest weight. He eats what he wants and when he wants within reason. He doesn't get too crazy with it and has some pretty good self-control when it comes to snacks and sweets. He's getting back active in the church again with the choir, congregational care, and missionary society. Dad loves being active in church in any area that may need help. From the ministering in the choir, to welcoming guests, to volunteering with Meals on Wheels, he stays active in the church. He's always encouraging and praying for others and topping it off with a joke to make them smile. Church work is a joy for him, and it fuels his energy and spirit. My parents are the reason why I stay active in church because they show me how using our specific talents and gifts in church helps to support the church's mission and do what's pleasing to God. Supporting ministries within the church not only strengthens the church body, but it also strengthens our relationship with God. Mom always said, "Only what you do for Christ will last." She's right, but sometimes I just want to sleep in. My parents encouraged so many people within our church just by living their life and gave hope to those who experienced health challenges themselves.

As Dad continued to work in various ministries in our church, he eventually became good friends with a young couple that recently joined First Missionary Baptist and started becoming more active in church activities. The GCs enjoyed seeing Dad at church and interacting with him and his encouraging spirit. They became good friends and shared stories of their experiences in college, in a fraternity, and in life. As their friendship grew, Mom and I became fond of the couple as well. I didn't talk to them much, but felt they were a nice, genuine couple.

Unfortunately, the GCs received bad news about Mr. GC's health since he was recently diagnosed with cancer. The conversations between my dad and Mr. GC transformed from lighthearted jokes to serious advice on how to navigate through cancer. As he told my dad about his journey of learning the type of cancer he had, information about the procedure, and the various doctors he's working with, my dad was giving him beneficial advice. He told him about the good vs bad doctors and how the red devil will make you feel from start to finish. They exchanged experiences with various symptoms and how their bodies reacted to cancer. It's like they were exchanging war stories to see who survived the illness the best. Mr. GC let us know when he will have surgery and his total recovery time before he's back to normal. As a family, we kept him and his wife in our prayers as they navigated the road we had traveled many times before. They're nervous but liked the fact that they can confide in us, especially my dad, about their feelings and reservations with their cancer diagnosis. Dad is in full ministry mode at this point, quietly but effective.

It seems like a couple of months go by and Mr. GC comes to church happy and healthy. He's lost a little bit of weight, but that's to be expected. Mr. GC has his same friendly and comedic personality as before and you could tell he's glad that God walked with him during his ordeal. Mr. GC takes the time to always thank my dad for ministering to him and encouraging him throughout the whole process. He said my dad is the reason why he not only went through with the procedure but felt confident enough that he would be ok. He felt that since my dad survived his blood cancer, that he would survive his cancer journey as well. Mr. GC and his wife are glad to have survived that ordeal and began to focuson having a family.

During the whole interaction between the GCs and my dad as they shared cancer war stories, I just watched and listened in the background and felt inspired by my dad's faith and trust in God being reflected on other people in the church. It was interesting to watch, and I learned how his life was a blessing to others....

Until the GCs started having children. The GCs survived cancer and now they have the nerve to have children. This bothered me to my core! Why? Because I was jealous. YES, I WAS JEALOUS! So, my dad goes through cancer (TWICE), loses his immune system, deals with not being able to work, and has to get a bone strengthening treatment every month to live a somewhat normal life just to end up encouraging someone to live a better life than him? Mr. GC gets cancer, survives it, and then continues living life like nothing happened? I mean I'm glad he's doing well, and the Lord healed him, but what about my dad? This GC couple is going on trips, having children, singing in the choir and living life just as happily as they can be, and I was livid! I knew Mr. GC was 20 years younger than my dad but come on Lord. You didn't spruce up my dad like you did Mr. GC! And I don't like it. So, what do I do? I hold a grudge and let that anger sit in a special corner of my heart labeled "GC". I'm sitting here watching them enjoy all the experiences of their life that I felt my dad should be enjoying too. Why can't my dad be that energetic again? Why does Mr. GC get one bout of cancer, but my dad gets two? The questions I had I knew they were selfish, arrogant, un-Christ like, distasteful, and mean, but I didn't care at the time. I was mad! And that anger stayed between me and God for a LONG time. I didn't tell anyone about it because I knew my jealousy didn't make sense and I really didn't feel like explaining it to anyone. Also, I just wanted to be angry at someone for my frustration and didn't feel like listening to someone tell me "Monica, that's not right." I already knew it wasn't right, but it's what I felt! Whenever Mr. GC interacted with me at church, I was still cordial and nice to him, but internally I was fuming. The experience and interactions were a teachable moment:

Year 1 of GC anger

Lord, what was the point of having my dad go through so much sickness just to restrict his body even more?

The Lord is silent.

While attending a church activity for the youth, Mr. GC came to talk to me as usual. We see each other weekly so we're having to regularly interact. He gives me his usual warm greeting of "Hey Monica, how's it going? How's your father doing?" Internally I'm wondering why he doesn't just talk to my dad himself, but I don't say that out loud. I told him "It's going well. Dad's doing pretty good."

"Good, tell him I asked about him."

"Sure will" I said as I'm walking away and trying not to give him the side eye.

The anger continues into the second year.

Year 2 of GC anger

Lord, why couldn't my dad live a fulfilling life with his family and continue to do what he wants to do?

The Lord is silent.

Again, attending another church event and Mr. GC comes to talk to me as usual. There's no point in trying to avoid him without it looking like I'm crazy.

Here we go with the conversation again. He happily says, "Hey Monica. Your son is growing up so fast."

Of course I'm internally thinking that's what children do, they grow, but I keep my snarky words to myself and just responded with "Yep, time is going by fast."

"How's your father doing?"

I really wanted to tell him "You should know, aren't you his friend?" But I restrained myself and told him, "He's doing well, getting ready to work the church picnic."

"Tell him I said Hey. He has been such an inspiration to me and my family. Always encouraging."

"Sure will."

This goes on for another year.

Year 3 of GC anger

Lord, why are you having Mr. GC interact with me? We have 2,512 members in this church, and you make it a habit of him talking to me. He's living the life that my dad should be living so why is GC talking to me? Lord......

The Lord is silent.

Another church event and I'm having another interaction with Mr. GC.

"Hey we should get our families together sometime and have dinner before our second one comes along."

I wanted to yell "NO" but "Sure, I'll let Mom and Dad know" is all that comes out.

"Great, we'll set a date."

"Great."

Beginning of Year 4 of GC anger

Lord why is it....

The Lord firmly interrupts me with, **"I don't have to tell you anything. What I have planned for your father is your father's story. It has nothing to do with you. Look at your father. He has lived a fulfilling life. Look at your sister, she's living a full life. Look at you, you're living a full life. Your father has already raised you and your sister, and you both are raising your own children. So, your father has lived. His life is not about you, but about the whole picture that you refuse to see. I know the reason for his life, and I don't have to tell you."**

Now I'm the one that's silent.

I stayed quiet for a few days about the matter because the Lord shut me up. I quickly learned that I was being selfish because I felt that my dad should be living a life that I thought he should have and not realizing he had already lived. My dad has done the things that Mr. GC was living through now as he was growing his family. I felt the Lord owed me some sort of explanation due to my own limited understanding. I only saw the situation from my point of view, not how my dad's life was a blessing to others. No wonder my prayers weren't getting answered. They weren't prayers, they were complaints. I was too busy complaining about what I thought my dad didn't have instead of being grateful for the things my dad already accomplished. I guess part of me wanted my dad to be the energetic father that I saw Mr. GC being to his child. I had to remind myself that God knows what to do because he sees the whole picture and my perspective did not matter. All I had to do was trust that God's plan benefits everyone including my dad and blessings aren't just limited for my dad. I wasted three whole years being angry, for what? Why did I let it bother me so much?

I learned two valuable lessons during my anger. First, as a caregiver I'm going to get mad at the fact that my loved one is suffering. I was mad because I felt that my parents don't deserve to be sick and how could God let them endure something beyond their control. I'm mad because their sickness affects me and the family and there's nothing we can do but let the storm run its course. I'm mad because the timing of their sickness is never right, and it seems like God isn't listening to me when I pray. I'm mad because I'm human and it's a reflection of my love and empathy. I was mad and it was ok. I just had to go through my anger to understand my emotions and learn to stop boxing God's will into what I thought it should be. Seeing things just from my perspective is not how God sees things and it's not how he operates.

Second, I learned to always be kind to others because I have no idea what people are going through personally. Even though he never knew my feelings, Mr. GC always treated me with kindness and respect even though he never knew I was angry. I was never angry with him directly because he never did anything wrong. He and his family were completely innocent and blameless. I was just angry about my dad's condition and took my feelings out on him. Mr. GC was just grateful that my dad was around to give advice and be an encourager. My anger was personal and had nothing to do with Mr. GC. So be kind to people. You never know what they had to go through just to show up. Everything is not about me and therefore if I see someone with an attitude, I don't take it personally. They could just be in a disagreement with God and don't know how to navigate it.

My thoughts and behaviors have changed since then. I consider the whole picture of every situation in my life and think about how it will affect me in the future instead of just on that day. I trust God more with the storms and inconveniences in my life since I know that he has already worked them out; I'm just going through it. And I don't take my life or my family's life for granted. Each one of our lives is a blessing to ourselves and to others who we may or may not know they're watching. It's not about us, it's about the body of Christ that work together to encourage each other in song and prayer.

Now, I give myself the opportunity to sit in my feelings and learn from them. Not for three years though, that was too long and ended up giving me too many gray hairs.

But if you harbor bitter envy and selfish ambition in your hearts, do not boast about it or deny the truth.

– James 3:14 NIV

Chapter 8: Blessings Can't Be Blocked

From my observation, the food we eat plays a major role in our overall health. It takes a long time to reverse or slow down the harsh effects that fried, greasy food has on our bodies. For years, my family has eaten whatever we wanted just like everyone else does. So, when it comes to changing our diet and eating healthier, it's mainly because our family must watch for high cholesterol, diabetes, and high blood pressure that runs in the family. We don't overindulge, but we do watch our intake of sweets, fried chicken, hamburgers, ribs, and pizza. Over time, our bodies tell us when there's something wrong that needs immediate correction. It gives us little warning signs, sort of like a check engine light, to let us know when our intake is getting out of hand.

There are days when Dad gets tired and there are days when Dad stays tired. After recovering from the red devil and Multiple Myeloma, Dad was able to work again once he gained approval from his doctors. But he was only able to work part-time since his doctors knew that he physically and medically could not work full-time demanding work hours, regardless of the type of job. So naturally, I think he's tired from his part-time job because rebuilding his body while trying to make an income three days a week is a lot to handle. He gets tired and winded more often than before, but that's just part of work life, right?

The tiredness becomes more of an inconvenience and Dad decides to talk to his cardiologist about it, as suggested by Mom. Mind you, Mom and Dad have THE BEST cardiologist that North Alabama or even the Southeast region of the U.S. has to offer. Their cardiologist gives suggestions to improve health, not just to sell you some procedure that won't be effective, so my parents trust his direction and expertise. Thank God for blessing doctors with the knowledge and capabilities to improve the health of others.

During his routine visit with his cardiologist, Dad goes through tests to figure out the cause of his tiredness and shortness of breath. Come to find out, he has some blockage in his arteries and by some, I mean 80 percent of blockage. No wonder the man was tired! His heart can barely get enough blood to it. So, here's another medical procedure I get to learn about. When there's blockage in the arteries, the doctors have a way of clearing that blockage to make an open pathway for blood to flow freely that helps the heart operate. To clear that blockage, doctors must put in mesh-like stints to open the artery and get the blood flowing again. This is all new to me, so I rely on my sister's medical expertise to learn how all this goes. Dad will have this procedure fairly quickly to help his heart perform better and get Dad back to some normalcy. It seems like our family has become besties with the hospital and medical facilities and it is not cute. Of course, Dad's cardiologist scheduled the procedure, talked us through the process, and suggested a healthier diet and exercises to help his heart perform better. Mom, sister, and I coordinated our schedules on who's going to stay at the hospital with him, who's going to bring lunch, and who's going to come by at night if he has to stay overnight in the hospital. We ran through our schedules and prepared for his procedure within the next few days. At the same time, I'm preparing for an interview at my job that could lead to a promotion.

I had been working in the financial industry for about four years leading up to Dad's heart procedures. During those four years, I was able to have a couple of promotions and as a reflection of my work performance, dedication, and results, it was time for another promotion. But this one would be a game changer for me. Double the pay, more opportunities for investment strategies, and opportunities for higher bonuses. Whew Lord thank YOU for directing my career path because I wanted to be financially comfortable for my son and me! This promotion meant so much to me, but Dad's procedure was on my mind heavy as well. Why? Because his procedure and my interview for the promotion were on the same day at the same time. Yep, the Lord's timing is perfect, but I thought it was way off this time. The questions running through my mind while preparing for my interview were "What situation have I resolved recently that produced quality results? How did 80 percent blockage come up out of nowhere? Do I need to change my diet? How much of my performance contributed to investment dollars for the quarter? How to I cultivate and manage profitable relationships? What's my value proposition? How big are the stints that go in your arteries? So, this is heart disease? Do I wear black or blue for my interview?" Needless to say, it was a long week, but as it got closer to my interview and Dad's procedure, I learned that God already blessed the doctors to handle this procedure with care as they have done millions of times before and if it's my time for a promotion, then it's my time. I started to become more at peace with the situations because the more I stressed about it, the less productive I became, which effected my results.

Finally, Thursday came around and it was time for my interview. I decided to wear my black suit with a green blouse and my black patent leather pumps. I always wear green for interviews because to me it means "it's a go" and no matter what the outcome is, I still accomplished something. I get to work, and my interview is scheduled for the afternoon while Dad's procedure is scheduled for 11:30am. Every hour leading up to my interview, I replayed my answers over and over in my head to be sure I included qualitative details and my performance measures. Then 11:30am comes and I pray,

"Lord, you know what is needed to heal my father so bless the doctors and cardiologists to complete this procedure with ease as they always do and repair the damage in Dad's arteries. Please protect my father during his procedure and bless the doctor's hands to be able to clear up his blockage, install a solution, and not find NOTHING ELSE going wrong in there. Bless that all will go well, and he comes out better than before. And calm mom's nerves because you know she can't handle stress. Just get me through this interview and in Your will, let me earn this promotion. Thank you for this position and for this job opportunity. Amen."

I cleared my mind and walked into my interview with confidence. While Dad was getting stints placed into his chest, I was in the middle of qualifying my performance to justify my promotion. This interview was a break or make moment since I kind of bombed the pre-screening phone interview because apparently, I'm not bubbly enough over the phone. For the entire hour of the interview, I just focused on providing qualified answers and acted like I already had the position. For that one hour, I blocked everything out and gave my best answers. After I left out of the office at the conclusion of my interview, I went back to my desk and immediately reached out to my sister to see how Dad was doing and if Mom was fussing at the hospital staff yet. Dad was doing well and sitting up talking and asking how we were feeling. He was feeling like himself again and the doctors kept him overnight just as a precaution and then he'd be home. After work, I went to pick my son up from school and we headed to the hospital to lay eyes on Dad. We walked in to see that he was holding up well post procedure. I asked him "So how are you feeling?"

"Doing better now. The procedure went pretty well. How are YOU doing?"

"We're doing pretty good, not a bad day. I see you like hanging out in the hospital now."

"Yeah, they sort of like me around here. But I'll be out soon and back to normal."

Mom is relieved that the whole ordeal is over, and we continue to talk about the rest of the week and Dad's change in diet. She mentioned that the hospital food that they've been giving Dad has been bland and nasty, but that's to be expected due to the procedure he just had. Mom started complaining about the food and says, "They don't put any seasoning on this food."

"Well, he did just have blockage in his arteries" I responded.

"They can at least put some salt and pepper on it."

"Ma'am

We continued to stay with him for some more hours and waited for sister to get off work and come up to the cardiology floor after her shift. We talked as a family about the next steps and began to make our way home. Another successful procedure in the books.

One week passed and as it turns out, the interview went well, and the management team was impressed with my responses and work ethic. I got the promotion, and I will be starting my new position within two weeks. Look at God! More money, a new location, and a new challenge that I'm ready for. I was so excited and grateful that I was able to accomplish another feat. This promotion meant being taken out of my comfort zone again, but it will definitely be worth it. I told my parents about my interview and promotion, and they are proud of me which means a lot. They asked about the new location I'll be at and some of my new responsibilities. Besides giving them the details, I was glad that both Dad and I had positive outcomes to our situations.

Two weeks have passed and I'm getting more comfortable in my new position and I'm loving my new paycheck. Another promotion was in the books so it's time for a celebration! I called sister and told her, "Sister, we're going to Nashville to celebrate!! My treat!!" Sister and I are always down for some foolishness, so it doesn't take much for us to decide to have fun. We take a quick trip to Joe's Crab Shack in Nashville and indulge in crab legs and drinks the whole night. We talked about my career path, our parents, my next goals, and our next trip location. It feels good to celebrate the victories and not always focus on what's going wrong. We needed these little get away trips to remind us to enjoy life and take advantage of every opportunity.

This trip would lead to many more "sister trips" away from family and responsibilities. What's life without some fun!

Cast all your anxiety on Him because He cares for you.

−1 Peter 5:7 NIV

Chapter 9: Coordination, please!

Cancer is bad itself without having all the long-term side effects. After enduring the red devil, prescriptions, and procedures, you still have to be mindful of the side effects. And these side effects aren't just minor like headaches, night sweats, or mood changes; they're more like heart disease, memory loss, strokes, bone density and more. It's like "Congrats! You survived cancer, now prepare to dodge every flying bolder that's thrown at you!"

It's 2016 and Mom has now been a 20-year breast cancer survivor by this time and has maintained relatively good health. She keeps up with her sugar levels since she has diabetes and eats her meals on schedule to coordinate with her prescriptions. Diabetes runs in our family, so we have to watch what, when, and how we eat. Unfortunately, diabetes causes heart disease, so Mom regularly gets checked out to keep an eye on things, such as cholesterol, blood sugar, and blood pressure levels. There are times when she gets too tired with fluctuating energy levels throughout the week or sometimes throughout the day. When it comes to her health, Mom cannot stand it when she doesn't feel good. Whether it's a cold, flu, neuropathy, headache, or stomachache, she just wants it to be over especially since her pain tolerance level is VERY low. She starts to notice that her energy level is lower and can't do as much as she used to throughout the day. There are times when she can't get out the bed or she has trouble getting up and down the stairs in their house. Her chest feels tight at times, and she can barely sleep through the night. I thought it was a side effect of breast cancer and suggested that she exercised more. I told her, "Maybe exercising some throughout the day to build up your endurance more."

"I do exercise some" she says in a way where she's trying to convince me of her opinion of exercising.

"WHEN?!"

"I walk around the school when taking the students back and forth to their scheduled activities."

"That's not exercising. That's normal walking around."

She doesn't listen to my advice, but that's to be expected. Her chest pains start to get more inconvenient and she decided to visit her doctor who is again the best cardiologist in North Alabama. She met with her cardiologist, and they decided to do a series of stress tests. Two separate appointments are scheduled; one for her actual stress test and another to review her results. Whenever Mom has an appointment with a specialist, I usually take her because it normally requires her to have a designated driver. Now her appointments are never on the days that are convenient to my 9-5 work schedule, so I typically have to rearrange some things around.

Mom called me and said, "Um, Monica. I need you to take me to my doctor's appointment at 8:30a on Tuesday."

"Doctor's appointment for what?"

"It's for a stress test to check what's going on with my heart. I need to find out what's going on because I shouldn't be this tired. So can you take me?"

"Is that the only day and time they have available. I've got a meeting at work at that time."

"Just tell them it's for a doctor's appointment. They should excuse you for that. It won't take long."

"It doesn't work like that……. I'll just take you."

For some odd reason, parents set appointments before confirming they have a ride or considering the time of day. They set all these appointments then call and say "you have to take me on this day at this time" instead of asking what does work best for everyone's schedule. Yes, early morning appointments are best, but appointments never last only an hour. There's at least an hour worth of round-trip travel time within the city to and from the appointment plus a 30-minute wait to see the doctor plus an hour to converse with the doctor then check out time to discuss prescription for medication or follow up information. So, taking someone to an appointment really means being out of the office for at least three hours of the day. Then who really wants to go back to work after a morning full of errands and doctor's appointments? I can either request a personal day off or come to work late and skip having a lunch. I talked with my manager and decided that I will come to work late instead of taking a whole personal day. Working a half day on Tuesday would mean working a half day on Saturday to make up for the hours I missed to still get 40 hours that week. I do this because I want my 40-hour paycheck, not a 34-hour paycheck. If I don't do anything else at work, I keep up with my work hours, my paycheck dollars, and my vacation days. Don't play!

On Tuesday, I get up at 6:15a.m. to get ready, pick Mom up from their house, and head to her doctor's appointment that's at 8:30a.m. We pulled up to the office and I let her out while I went to find a park. Mom never likes where I park so I've learned to just drop her off at the entrance and find my parking spot in peace. I waited in the lobby for her to finish her appointment and give me an update. It took a little longer than an hour for her to finish up and I could tell she was worn out. She spoke to the receptionist to discuss her follow- up appointment and what to expect going forward. After two hours had passed, she was done with the doctor, and I pulled the car around for her. Now our car rides are quite hilarious since this gives Mom a chance to tell me all the details while we gossip about daily foolishness. I've learned that car rides are the best therapeutic and hilarious activities for our family and serve as a safe space for thoughts, emotions, and critical thinking. She gets in the car and our regular routine starts. I started off by saying "Girl, you looked tired. What did they have you doing in there?"

"Some of everything! I had to walk on the treadmill and do other exercises all at one time. I feel like I've ran a mile! I hope they're able to find out what's going on after all this work they had me doing."

"When will you find out the results?"

"I've got to come back down here in a couple of weeks to find out. And they better not make me pay another copay. Today with all the work I've done it better be waived. Lord, it's just so much going on!"

"It's ok, He's already worked it out. Lord, I hope they don't charge you a copay."

I dropped her back off at home after picking up breakfast and I checked to see how Dad's doing before I headed back to work. I finished my workday at 5:30p and I headed home to cook some dinner. Thankfully, my son is already at home after riding the bus from school and I ask about how his day went while preparing a quick meal. Once we eat dinner, review his homework, and get ready for the next day, I spend the next few hours working on my small business. Yes, I manage my own small business part-time that helps other small business owners with business development strategies to achieve their growth potential locally and nationwide. So, working a full-time job and managing my business part-time has definitely been a balancing act these past few years, but I enjoy it. Having time management has become an important aspect to manage each segment of my life while being a mother, a daughter, and an employee without somehow exhausting myself. How do I make the time and not go crazy? I just make time for what I need to make time for and take it day by day. Not everything needs to be managed and done in one day.

A couple of weeks pass, and Mom gets feedback from her cardiologist on her stress tests. Her performance is not where it should be, and they want to continue running more tests. She's not happy about it and finds it to be an inconvenience, but she follows directions anyway. She goes through more testing and comes to find out she has blockage in her arteries too. They also noticed that her heart beats are just off, irregular. Random, raggedy heart beats. So, to clear the blockage, Mom must have stints placed in her arteries as well, along with needing a pacemaker to manage her heart rate. We found out that a new medical advancement will allow her pacemaker to send daily updates to her doctor about her heart's performance using Bluetooth technology.

This way, medical teams can monitor any changes in her heart rate without her leaving home or constantly having to visit the doctor every week. Of course, this all requires a procedure and Mom is nervous about all that is going on with her heart. After learning about the procedure, her new equipment, and her need to change her diet, I immediately asked my parents,

"You all couldn't coordinate this better? Your timing is so off, like can we get a break in between these procedures. Clearly you all didn't plan this efficiently. Whew Jesus! Just running your children down through there!"

These back-to-back illnesses are getting a little out of hand. Lord, I know your time is not our time, but this time it seems like it's all over the place. And Mom is just beside herself about having this procedure. Dad was more optimistic about his heart procedure while Mom was more panicky. The first things she said was "Lord, I didn't know my heart was so weak. Just in case, my life insurance policy is in the file cabinet downstairs with all our burial information."

"Wait now, it's not THAT bad. This is something routine" as Dad responded in a calming voice.

"Anything could happen when they start messing with your heart."

I told her, "Girl, you're not going anywhere. You're still going to be fussing at folks once the procedure is done. They're not replacing your whole heart; they're just putting something in there to help it perform better. You'll be alright."

"Lord my daughter doesn't take nothing serious. Her mother is preparing for a major procedure and she's playing."

"I'm dead serious. You think you survived cancer just to lose to a heart monitor."

"Right!" Dad says in agreement.

Mom continues to tell us about her medical records, burial policy and life insurance information. This is an important conversation to have and as a family we have talked about end-of-life paperwork and processes since it is a necessary and vital conversation to have. Not preparing your family for the end of life does a disservice to your loved ones and leaves them frustrated with legal processes instead of taking the time to grieve. I'm glad that Mom feels comfortable with having discussions about life insurance, sickness, burial policies, and what she wants included in her obituary because it's all vital information to help make the transition smoother. But must it be the first solution to every sickness? Ma'am! The heavens aren't calling your name today.

Since Dad just had stints placed in his arteries and slowly recovering, he's not able to help Mom 100% with her recovery cause he's still building his strength back up. Sister is trying to keep the hospital from burning up since they act like they can't survive without her managing it every minute. Again, she saves people's lives, I save people's money. With all that's going on with the parentals and to prevent losing my job for the days I would need to come to work late or having to leave early to help my parents out, I decided to take advantage of FMLA. I wasn't up to date on how FMLA works, but I took the time to figure it out since I had that resource available.

And yes, I did my research on company time. I learned that FMLA would allow me to be absent from work as needed without it being counted against my performance or attendance which relieved some of my stress from trying to figure out how to be two places at once using virtual options. In addition to FMLA, I get one paid week of time off to use for medical reasons such as recovering from a sickness or taking care of an immediate family member. So, I get the paperwork ready to take to Mom's next doctor's appointment and have the cardiologist fill it out and get it approved for the paid week off. I submitted it back to the third-party insurance company at work and after two long weeks, they finally confirmed that I could be off with pay and will start processing payroll for that week off. Now sending the paperwork and getting paid are two different things. It only took two weeks to fill out the paperwork, gain approval and have it processed. On the other hand, it took NINE months for me to get paid for ONE week! NINE MONTHS!! Complete unnecessary foolishness! Thank God I wasn't hurting for money too bad, or it would've thrown me way behind. By this time, we're one week away from Mom's procedure.

I told Mom about me taking the week for her procedure and to help her and Dad out around the house. She was so grateful for the help and kept telling me that the Lord would add days to my life. Mentally, I thought this would be a mini staycation for me as well to give me a break from work. Mom and I discussed the time she needs to be ready for her appointment and any chores that would need to be completed around the house during the week. We have our game plan set and we're ready to tackle the week ahead. Her appointment isn't until Tuesday, so I take advantage of sleeping in on Monday and enjoy a lazy day.

Thank God I did because unbeknownst to me, the rest of the week was about to be a mess!

On Tuesday, I get up at 5:30a.m. to get myself ready, clean my house up a little and head to pick Mom up for her appointment. I get to her house at 7:30a.m. assuming that she's ready, because after all this appointment is for her. It's 7:30a.m. and she's STILL in the shower getting ready for her 8a.m. procedure. I walk in the house yelling, "Ma! What are you doing?"

"I'm almost ready, just got to get my things together!"

"It's at 8a.m., right?"

"Yeah, it won't take me long."

I turned and asked Dad, "Dad, what has she been doing all this time?" All he could do was shake his head in disappointment.

It's now 7:43a.m. and we're just now leaving their house to head to her 8a.m. procedure that will take us 20 minutes to get to. Here's when the fun starts. I drop her off at the hospital entrance and she checks in while I parked the car. We waited a few minutes, and the medical staff took her back and prepared her for the procedure. We exchanged the typical "I love you" and I continued to wait in the lobby area of the cardiology floor. I got a chance to complete work for my small business while I waited for her to get done. After a couple of hours, she was done with the procedure and the doctors called me back to give an update. They gave me a run down on the procedure, how her pacemaker would work, and the equipment that she'll be going home with to help monitor her heart rate. I then get a chance to see her and called Dad to give him a rundown of how the procedure went and that she's doing well and is ready to eat. Of course, she will not like the hospital food but who does. I made sure she ate, and sister comes up to check on her and see how the operation went. The doctors are going to keep her overnight to watch her, then she'll go home the next day. I leave the hospital to take Dad something to eat and make sure their laundry is done. After I hung out with Dad, I headed home to start dinner before my son gets home from school in 30 minutes. I finish dinner, hear about his day at school then take him to his boy scout meeting at 6p.m. While he's in his meeting, I go pick up Mom and Dad's prescription, get a few groceries for my house then finish up in time to get my son from his meeting. We head back home where he starts his homework and I finish up some work for my small business. By the time I get to sleep it's 11:13pm.

I. Am. Tired.

It's Wednesday and I get up early again to get dressed and head back to my parents' house to have some breakfast with Dad. Dad and I ate breakfast while watching the local morning news and waited for the call to pick Mom up from the hospital. At 10a.m., she's discharged and ready to come home so I head to the hospital and pull to the front door so that the medical staff can load her into my car. Now for some reason, even though she's been in the hospital overnight, Mom has a million errands to run. Ma'am! She gets in the car and says, "Whew! Thank you for picking me up. You can't get any rest in the hospital because they bother you all hours of the night."

"Did they give you breakfast?"

"That nasty food! The eggs were bland, and the grits were cold. And they won't give you any sweet tea."

"Well. you just had stints put in…."

"Sweet tea ain't gonna hurt! Look, take me by Cracker Barrel to pick up breakfast. I want a real, hot meal so I can take my medicine. Then I need to go by Walgreens to pick up my prescription."

"I already picked it up…."

"This is my new prescription they just gave me at the hospital. That's all they do is give you more medicine. I feel like I have a whole pharmacy in my purse. I'm sick of all this medicine! And my insurance better pay for it!"

"Lord help. Look, you know you have new restrictions because of your procedure. They called me and let me know your post-op activities."

Mom said with a surprised face, "They called you too! Yeah, they told me about it but child, I'm going to go home, eat, and get in that bed to rest. They don't have to worry about me doing anything. Couldn't half rest in the hospital anyway."

I picked up her meal from Cracker Barrel, ran by the pharmacy to get her new medication, then we finally made it back to the parentals house. We get in and we give Dad the update on doctor's orders and the follow up appointment. I made sure they were ok then ran my own errands to pick up a few business supplies and paid my utility bill. I got back home in time to see my son get off the bus at 4:30p.m. to listen to his eventful day at school. We then went to church for Bible Study at 6:30p.m. My church is friendly, so I'm greeted by at least three people every Wednesday before Bible study starts. The first church member that greeted me wanted to get an update about Mom. They said, "Hey! I heard your mom had a procedure today. How's she doing?"

"She's well. She's back home resting now, but she's feeling good."

"Good! Tell her I asked about her."

I made it down the hallway a little before another church member wanted to check in on how Mom's procedure went. They asked, "How's your mother doing?"

"She's well. She's at home resting now."

"Tell her I said hello. Let us know if you all need anything."

Now, I'm finally heading to my Bible study class when another member approached me. They come in threes. "Hey, didn't your mom have a procedure or something today?" they asked.

"Yep, she's back home resting up. I'll let her know you asked about her."

"Yeah, let them know we're here if they need something. Your Dad doing alright?"

"Yep, he's taking it easy."

Sometimes as a caregiver, being asked the same question over and over again gets tiring, especially when we want a break from the constant reminder that we're taking care of someone. Our personal identities get lost while being a caregiver as we're seen as the informant, the closest family member, or just the caregiver.

People always asked "How are THEY doing? How can they help THEM? What are THEY up to?", but hardly ask "How are YOU doing? What do YOU need help with? How can I give YOU a break?" Sometimes I just want to tell them "If you want to know how they're doing, just call them. They'll be glad to hear from you!" Unfortunately, my tone will not match the innocence of that statement, so I give my normal response of "They're doing well. I'll let them know you asked about them." It's a sweet and straight to the point statement that's enough consolation for the both of us and allows the requester to feel good about their concern and check the box off. Congrats! You've checked on the family within one minute.

Bible study finishes up around 8p.m. and my son and I travel home for the night. I got home and called the parentals to see how they were doing and told them about who asked about them then had my usual late-night conversation with my son. He goes to sleep, and I tackle a few more business tasks before calling it a night. I end up going to sleep at 12:15a.m.

Lord, I have to be up in six hours. Please let this six-hour sleep feel like eight hours of rest so I can use YOUR strength tomorrow. Lord, thank you for the recovery and good health of my parents and the doctors who take care of them with their best interest in mind. Lord, thank you for healthy relationships in my family and those within the church body. Thank you for the opportunity to take time off work to take care of my parents while they recover. Thank you that my son is maturing and is enjoying school.......

....

Don't act like I'm the only one that falls asleep in the middle of a good prayer!

From going between my house, my parent's house, running errands, taking care of son, attending meetings, cooking dinner and running a small business, I was tired! That week WORE ME OUT! Managing two homes and three different people was a full-time job. JESUS! Between sister and I trading off tasks between the morning and the evenings, it was still a lot. Like, there's not a caregiver guide or scheduler for this kind of stuff because this is A LOT! But our parents recovered well and what seemed like a huge challenge turned out to be a relatively well-managed project. I felt like I needed another week off from work, but I went back to work that next week.

Juggling my own schedule along with helping my parents started to stretch me thin. Working full time, being a single mother, staying very active in my church, and running a small business quickly helped me realize that I needed to prioritize my time better and rearrange some things. I just KNEW I could do everything, but how? How was I going to organize my time that would help me balance everything. I didn't want to neglect anyone or any one of my priorities, but I had to be strategic with my time. I had to find my flow. But without realizing it, slowly I started to put myself last. Why? Because I wanted to be sure everything else was taken care of before I sat down.

I was dedicated to my family. Dedicated to my career. Dedicated to my church. Dedicated to my small business. Those wheels kept turning and I kept riding the road.

"You expected much, but see, it turned out to be little. What you brought home, I blew away. Why?" declares the Lord Almighty. "Because of my house, which remains a ruin, while each of you is busy with your own house…

-Haggai 1:9 NIV

Chapter 10: I Want to Buy a House!

"You going to buy a house by yourself?"

"You're not going to wait to get married to buy a house?"

"Ain't a man supposed to buy you a house?"

"You're ready for that?"

"Who told you to buy a house?"

The reason for telling people that I wanted to buy a house was so they could give me encouragement or advice or maybe just be happy for me. Sometimes people can ask the silliest questions. Therefore, you can't tell everyone everything.

Years ago in 2010, I invested some money in stock because one day I knew I wanted to buy a house, but I just wasn't mentally, financially, or emotionally ready for one at that time. I kept adding money to my investment to buy more stock, you know just $50 here, $100 there and so on. Well, now it's 2019 and time for me to cash in on it. I finally got tired of renting and having a small space that I couldn't decorate like I wanted. I was ready for a huge backyard and a garage because the Lord knows that my biggest pet peeve is scraping ice off my windshield. I missed living in a neighborhood and wanted to grill in the backyard without it being illegal. I had a better income at this time and worked on my credit to clean it up and achieve a better score. My credit score was finally a 645, just enough to get qualified for a house. I wasn't living paycheck to paycheck anymore and I wanted to prove to my son, and myself, that I could buy a house on my own. Well, one day I told my son to get in the car and we started riding around different neighborhoods to look at houses. I asked him what kind of house he wanted, not knowing that he has very expensive taste. This boy ONLY looked at two story, $500,000 houses for consideration. I had to tell him, "Son, these houses are expensive!"

"Well, I want stairs in a big house. Plus, a yard. In a nice neighborhood."

"Bet! But let's bring the price down, son. I'm all we got!"

A starter home or rancher was obviously beneath him even though he didn't have two dollars to contribute to the whole operation. I kept thinking "Who raised you!?" Keep in mind, children are just a reflection of ourselves. It's like watching me grow up again because just like him, I wanted a house with stairs too.

Anytime I decided to do something or make a major decision in my life, I remember my Dad's advice: run the numbers! He would say run the numbers and if it makes sense then go for it. If it doesn't then find another solution. I ran my numbers, and I knew how much I could comfortably afford for a monthly mortgage and how much house I wanted. Even though I knew I could pay rent, in the back of my mind I kept questioning if I could afford a mortgage. A four-bedroom house with a $1200 mortgage vs a small two-bedroom apartment with a $950 rent payment should be an easy feat, right? I had to make these numbers make sense or else it wasn't going to work. My mission was to move out of the city and more into the county for more yard space and quiet nights. After running my numbers to match my preference of a four-bedroom house with a huge backyard in the country, I reached back out to a prospective realtor that I met the previous year at work. I told him I was ready to finally buy a house and wanted to get the ball rolling. We scheduled a consultation of what I wanted and how much I wanted my mortgage to be and compared other neighborhoods. He informed me of aspects to consider when looking for my home and to keep an open mind. After all, the housing market was booming, and houses were quickly going under contract. We connected with one of his preferred lenders and discussed what I needed to get pre-qualified. I quickly learned that there's no point in looking for a house without having a pre-qualification letter in hand. Some things I had to be aware of, which included my student loan balance, my business income, and how it affects approvals, but that's another book for another day. God forbidden student loans and I'm STILL not using my degree!

After going over my credit score, income, and outstanding debt, I get my pre-qualification for a $300,000 house. Now to me, the lender was being really rude because why would you say I can afford a $300,000 house! I know for a fact that I can't afford that, and I don't want that kind of mortgage. Yes, the Lord has riches in glory that far exceed my imagination, but I'm not going to get greedy. I'm going to be reasonable and strategic and look for houses that are less than $200,000. My realtor and I decided on a time and date to start house hunting and we started the process. Here is when I get to know my realtor well and feel comfortable that he has enough expertise to guide me in the right direction without an ulterior motive. We went looking at houses and most of them, I didn't like it mainly because of the floor plan. Why on earth would someone want to walk into their house and the first thing to their right or left is a bedroom or bathroom with a huge window?

My preference was to have all the bedrooms towards the back of the house and my living room and dining room to be separate. And by separate, I mean a wall or kitchen separating them, not some random pillar or the back of a love seat separating the rooms. Floor plans nowadays are mainly great rooms or bedrooms located in the front of the house and I was NOT impressed. Just give me a traditional floor plan and I'll take it from there.

The houses I chose with a more favorable floor plan were bought so fast it was gone before I could even get my offer in. We kept looking and looking, but I just wasn't sold on one yet no matter how far out in the country we went. I was getting a little discouraged because I kept thinking that maybe it wasn't my time to purchase a home yet. Maybe this was God's way of saying I'm going in the wrong direction or doing something that He hasn't blessed yet. But I just wouldn't give up so easily. So, one Sunday morning in March, out of frustration, I drove around the county looking for random subdivisions and new homes popping up to get a feel of what I wanted. After driving around for over an hour, I finally found a subdivision that caught my eye that I remembered seeing six months prior. I drove through the subdivision and liked the layout of the neighborhood and multiple entrances. I saw people walking around the neighborhood or riding bikes to enjoy the nice sunny weather. I made a loop around the neighborhood and pulled next to the model home to check it out. I entered the model home quietly so I wouldn't be noticed walking through and looking at the decorated rooms. I didn't want anyone trying to talk me into buying the home, I just wanted to experience it on my own. After less than a minute at the home I fell in love with the layout.

This is it! This is the layout I want! Finally, someone gets it! I stood in the family room and started picturing where I would put my TV, new couches and reading area. I was in my own little world for a minute or two until I went to speak to a representative. I questioned the number of homes, and the current floor plans available, and the rep told me that there was a home being built with the same floor plan right down the street. The concrete had already been poured and the frame was up. I told the builder I wanted it! I called my realtor and said, "I found my home!"

"Wonderful. Where's it at? What's the address?"

"Here's the address. It's in the county and my son gets to stay in the same school zone!"

My realtor looks up the address and says, "Wait, this house isn't finished. You want this one?"

"Yep!"

"Sight unseen?! I don't know, that's kind of risky."

"It has the same floor plan as the model home, so yeah, I want it. I see what the result is going to be."

"Ok…. I'll trust your decision. We can look at more homes just in case."

"Nope! I want this one."

Let's get you in it."

The paperwork starts and the wheels are turning, and I never ran so fast to the bank to hurry up and put down my $1,000 earnest money. This house is MINE! I'm getting this house!

I'm so excited and nervous at the same time. Like everyone SIT DOWN! THIS IS SERIOUS. I'm buying a house. A single mother barely running her small business is buying a house. Here I am buying a house, and I can't believe it's actually happening. After a week of paperwork, I drove by the house under construction for the first time to see it in person. The frame was up, the water heater was going in, and I heard all the construction workers hammering and sawing away. It was a beautiful sound and sight for me. For the next six months, I would drive to this house just to look at it, check on the building process, and make sure all was going well. Seeing it go from a concrete slab to a solid frame, then to the appliances being put in was so rewarding. The closer it was getting to being completed, the more excited I became. I had my first approval, my house was coming close to being done, and I was ready for the smooth transition from apartment to house.

Now that the house is almost finished, it's now time to get ready to close. Yep, the financial road to home ownership. First, I cashed out my investment which grew enough for a good down payment on my first home. I learned that I didn't have to count it as additional income since it was going towards my first home purchase. Thank goodness I invested that money when I wasn't ready cause it came in handy now. My lender and title company gave me the run down on how much my down payment would be and all the closing costs, so I made sure to keep those funds set aside. I can check the down payment money off the long to do list.

Second, talking with the lender to figure out my financial fitness was so frustrating. I worked in the financial industry, so I knew my debt-to-income ratio, how to calculate it, and my ability to afford a mortgage loan. But midway through the process, my lender kept reporting my DTI inaccurately. Their calculation had me waiting another six months to close in order to pay off an auto loan, get another bonus from work, AND pay down my student loan. Excuse me! What changed within 30 days? I went back to run my numbers again to see what issues came up. My calculation along with their calculation was not adding up to be the same and as a Brokerage Associate, I know how to count and complete formulas. But between the lender and I, 2+2 was NOT equaling 4. So, I went to another financial institution for verification just to make sure I wasn't going crazy. I called the other financial institution and spoke to their point of contact for mortgage lending. When I went in, I simply asked them to calculate my DTI and tell me what it was. Guess what? I was right! My numbers matched their results to a tee. I thanked the rep for the information and left the office both mad and relieved. Now I'm calling my lender. I kindly said, "Hey, I'm follow up on the issue with my DTI."

"Yeah, we need to get it lowered so maybe paying off your car and lowering your student debt will help. The builder is willing to keep the house under contract for another three months until you're ready."

"And what do you show as my DTI again?"

"It's 55% which is way too high."

"I have it as 42%, because I have this amount of total debt in relation to this amount of income not counting my business income. So, after verifying it multiple times and reviewing the balances on my credit lines, you should show it as being 42% because nothing has changed within the past six months besides paying down debt. Even your competitor showed my DTI as 42% and I have proof of both my calculations and the competitor's."

"Let me run it again……….. You're right. Your DTI is 42%. I don't know how we got to 55%. Let me send this back to underwriting and get them to fix it."

"Don't even worry about it. It's been too many mistakes working with you and your underwriter so I'm going to go with another lender. Between losing my financial documents to miscalculating my DTI to giving me inaccurate mortgage information, I really don't want you all to handle my purchase anymore."

"I'm sorry that all this has happened to you and it's a mistake that should not have happened, but we will work to make it a smoother process. Do you really want to start all over?"

"I would rather start over in the right direction than continue as is in the wrong direction. Thank you for your time."

I let my realtor know the situation and he understood my reason for leaving. He suggested another lender that collaborates directly with my builder that would be willing to pay the closing costs. So, I ended up switching lenders in the middle of my home buying process. I let my new lender know of my upcoming closing in four weeks, and I immediately sent him all the required paperwork to get this ball rolling quickly. The constant copies of account statements, tax returns, paychecks and bonus checks started going back and forth again in order to meet the deadline. At one point I said,

I started this process without a house, and I will end this process without a house. You all are not going to stress me out about a house I'm not even in yet.

After a couple of weeks passed of me shuffling money around and finally receiving my pay from my week off for FMLA (yep, it took that long to get it. Exactly eight months later) and getting my documents together, I finally got the "clear to close" approval. JESUS! Those words sounded like gold after all the foolishness I've been through with this house. Now I'm getting closer to being in this house.

Third, all the appliances, cabinets, and electrical work was complete in the house and the last thing to work on was the landscape. I went by the house and the landscape was horrible. The landscapers literally just placed sod on top of an uneven yard that was not leveled or smoothed out at all. Gravel, large rocks, water bottles, and mud were all over my yard and they had the nerve to just lay sod on top like nothing was wrong. Just tacky. I had to get an engineer to come out and tell the landscapers and builder that the sides of the house had to be leveled down and even with the rest of the ground for water to drain efficiently to the backyard. There's a huge ditch in my backyard and apparently my yard serves as a swale to allow rainwater to run off into the ditch to make a natural lake in my backyard. Luckily there's nothing in my backyard besides a line of trees and a cotton field so the huge ditch isn't bothering anyone. I love the fact I have a huge, wide backyard, but this landscaping issue must be fixed. Plus, the engineer surveying my house realizes that the neighbor's fence was over on my property by over five inches. They either have to move it before I close on the house, or I would have to make them move it before seven years are up; otherwise, they can claim that part of my property as theirs. I know it's just five inches, but I want all the inches I paid for, so I told my realtor that I wanted their fence moved now. The neighbors agreed to move the fence, and this added another week to my closing date. My closing has moved three times now and living around boxes in my apartment was getting uncomfortable. And my landlord was tired of me changing my move-out date.

Lastly, they put the wrong carpet down in my house. How in the world do you put the wrong carpet down when I clearly chose gray, and this brown carpet looks nothing like gray. There were so many minor, inconvenient, and easily avoidable issues that just kept delaying the closing process.

Why so many delays?

Why are these minor issues happening?

Are the delays telling me I shouldn't buy this house?

Should I stop fighting for this house?

This is the time where I learned the difference between *"Be still and know that I am God"* and *"Faith without works is dead."* I kept wondering if this was God's way of seeing if I would keep fighting and working hard towards my blessing; or if this was a sign that I'm working towards the wrong house, the wrong goal. I wanted to give up SO MANY TIMES, but that was too easy. It was a cop out. So, after going back and forth on my prayers, my thoughts, and my doubts, I made the final decision that I've done too much and went through too much frustration to NOT get this house. I'm FIGHTING FOR IT!! My prayers went from *"Lord, should I just give up on this house because if it is your will for me to have it, then it wouldn't be this hard"* to *"I'm going to fight and get this house until you slap me in the face and say I can't have it."* This feels by far like the hardest thing I've ever done. The greatest feat I've personally had to fight. I'm emotionally and mentally over this home buying process.

My realtor called me and told me that the fence has been moved, the correct carpet has been laid, and the landscaping has been resolved. My new, final closing date is set for Tuesday, exactly one week away. I'm finally closing on my house!!

I had one week to pack up the rest of my things and get it all on the moving truck. On July 4th of 2019, I was busy packing boxes and loading furniture up on the moving truck as fast as I could. My son and I were sweating all day and missed out on eating some good barbeque. At last, Tuesday came, and it was the end of this long-lived saga. My closing is scheduled for 12 noon, so I left work early, went to the closing table, and got my keys! I had laid hands and prayed over this house alone so many times that it was so good to have it finally be mine. I would place my hand on the corner brick of my house during the building process and say, *"Lord please bless this house to be mine and let me create wonderful memories in it. You've built this house for me and now I need to move into it."* A four bedroom, two bath house with a huge backyard was mine! I got my U-Haul that was already loaded up and drove it to my new house. My parents met me there to congratulate me on my new home and helped my son and I move some things into the garage. Mom did her duty of praying over my house with holy oil as a way of blessing my house. It smelled like olive oil to me, but I'll take it. I was just glad to pull into

MY garage, open MY door, and walk through MY house all by the grace of God!!

It took a total of nine months for them to finish my home due to multiple rainy days, back orders of appliances, the wrong carpet being put in, and the ground not being leveled. Building my first new home was so interesting, but frustrating at the same time. A new build can have unexpected delays because things just go wrong or fall behind. So, the move out date from my apartment kept changing and I was steadily living around packed up boxes. And then there's the financial side of it. I'm just glad that the long scenario is over with.

The next day as I'm moving into my new home, I run by the parentals to get a few of my things I left at their house for temporary storage. I get there and Dad is relaxing in his recliner chair watching TV. He needed to rest because he had been helping me move some furniture off the U-Haul and into my new home. As I'm leaving their house, Dad walked me out to the car and lets me know that he's proud of me and all that I've done. I tell him that these folks ain't gonna kill me and we both laughed but Dad was laughing super hard. He laughed so hard that he cried. With water in his tear duct he said, "I can't stop laughing for some reason."

"Yeah, you're tickled!

"Well, I would come to your house, but I'm going to rest up some."

"Yeah, you get some rest because you've been doing a lot lately with helping me move and everything. Go rest and regroup.

Dad goes back into the house, and I head to my new home. Just my son and I in this big new house that we get to have fun in and decorate it just how we want it. We unpacked some more things then prepared to get ready for the next day since I have to work, and my son will be attending a summer program in the morning. Moving in the middle of the week is highly overrated and I do not suggest it all. My son and I got to sleep before waking up at 6:15a.m. the next morning. He's off to school and I'm at work when Mom calls me around 10:15a.m……....

Many are the plans in a person's heart, but it is the Lord's purpose that prevails.

-Proverbs 19:21 NIV

Chapter 11: The New Normal

Exactly two days later, 48 hours after my closing, my dad had a stroke……

Sister was on vacation in New Orleans.

I was moving things into my new house.

All while Dad was having a stroke.

The signs were there: uncontrollable laughter. Slurred speech. Loss of balance. Droopy face. Confusion.

One of the side effects of Multiple Myeloma is being more susceptible to strokes. Not just one, but multiple strokes could happen. They may be years or months apart, but they will happen. I noticed that Dad couldn't stop laughing, but laughter is one of his character traits, so I didn't think much of it. His balance was off, but this was normal since he's been using a cane daily now. He has a mass in his head that has affected his balance the past few years, so he's been using a cane to walk for a little while now. Either way, the signs of a stroke were there but I thought they were just amplified due to him helping me move. When I saw that he couldn't stop laughing, that's when he needed to go to the hospital. Instead, I told him to just go lay down. Overnight, his symptoms became worse. Mom noticed that Dad's speech became slurred and suggested he go to the hospital, but of course he declined and just waited to call his oncologist in the morning. By this time, it was 2a.m. in the morning and his face became droopy. By the time it's 7a.m., Dad is completely confused, and Mom tells him that he's going to the hospital.

This becomes a major stroke due to the delay in the time of getting it treated and the amount of damage it already caused. Strokes must be addressed within minutes, not hours, in order to prevent long-term damage. My family has been educated on the signs of stroke, but during these hours we don't act fast enough.

Of course, my mother was the first to notice his decline, but didn't realize what was going on as the hours passed. By the time they decided to head to the hospital, Dad could barely walk and was not 100% sure of what was happening or what was going on with his body. He just knew he couldn't control it anymore. Since he can't walk, she can't get him down the two flights of stairs in their home during the early morning hours. So, she called an ambulance. Keep in mind, Mom still hasn't called her daughters yet to tell us what's going on. The paramedics get to their house and after asking Dad questions and assessing his condition, they're able to lift him onto a stretcher and into the ambulance to finally get him to the hospital. But too much time has passed. Too many hours have gone by. Mom then calls me at 10:15a while I'm at work and tells me what happened during the night and the updates the doctors have provided. My whole mood changes. Towards the end of the conversation she says,

"Where's your sister? She's still out of town?"

"Yeah, but they're thinking about coming back here because of the hurricane coming towards New Orleans."

"Well don't tell her cause she'll have a fit. I don't want her worrying and trying to rush back. We'll just tell her when she gets back."

"No, she'll have a fit if we DON'T tell her. She's going to figure it out when she can't get in contact with Dad."

"Just wait to tell her."

I didn't listen to Mom, and I quickly called sister as soon as I hung up the phone with Mom. I called and said, "Sister, what are you doing?"

"Hey, we're still down here, but everyone is starting to load up and head back there because of the hurricane. All the events have been canceled so we're renting a car to come back instead of waiting on the train back to Birmingham."

"Goody. Look, have you talked to Dad?"

"I tried calling/texting him, but he hasn't responded. I don't know what's taking him so long to respond."

"Ok (exhales) Mom told me not to tell you, but Dad is at the hospital right now. He's had a stroke and he's been in the hospital since early this morning."

"WHAT??!!"

"Yep"

"When?"

"Some time last night. I saw him yesterday, and he was kind of off, but I thought he was just tired and having his dizzy spell again."

"Where is she!"

"Still at the hospital with him."

"……. I can't believe this…. I'm coming home NOW!!"

While Dad goes through testing at the hospital, the doctors confirmed that he's had a stroke and that he'll be in the hospital for a while to monitor him. The stroke affected the right side of his brain which has him completely paralyzed on his left side. COMPLETELY. This became a major stroke overnight quickly and caused major damage to his body. I'm devastated and sister is just torn to pieces about it. How in the world did our Dad have a stroke? I couldn't focus all day at work. I was there physically, but mentally I kept thinking that I was losing my Dad. The man who used to pick me up off the couch and carry me to my room and tuck me in my bed when I was little was now paralyzed. How?!

I get off work, go pick my son up from my house, and head to the hospital to see him. I looked at Dad and he had a different look on his face, but I couldn't let my concern show on my face. He's not the same and it's breaking my heart. To calm my thoughts and emotions, I asked him, "So you just wanted to come to the hospital today, huh?"

"You know, gotta keep these people in check."

"How do you feel?"

He then continues to tell me his perspective of what happened and how he was out of it for a moment and couldn't understand what was happening. Then he says, "But you know I'll be alright. I'll be out of here soon."

"So, you're paralyzed?"

"Yeah, but that's just temporary. Does your sister know yet?"

"Yep!"

"She's probably going to fuss."

"Oh, she's definitely going to fuss at you. I'm just the calm before the storm."

Talking with him gave me a little relief, but I knew things would be completely different going forward. At first, for an odd reason, I was not a complete emotional wreck when I first found out about my Dad's stroke. I was a bit numb to the reaction as if it was a dream or something minor. Maybe I didn't have any more emotions left in me after stressing about purchasing a new house, stress from my job, stress from making sure my finances would be ok, and stress from being a single parent. I had poured out so much emotion into my home and work that I was just drained. So, when my Dad had a stroke, it was more like "interesting" than a "OH MY LORD, WHAT IS HAPPENING!!"

Dad's talking to me like this situation is temporary and I believe that he believes it is temporary. But as the numerous days go by that he's in the hospital, we both learn that this is his new life. No getting up and leaving the hospital in two days. No eating and sleeping without interruption. No going to the bathroom alone. No more walking without help. No more living life like how he wants. I labeled this era of new life as Lamentations. In Lamentations, Jeremiah describes the horrible living conditions in Jerusalem after the Babylonians destroyed the city. Those who were left behind to continue living in Jerusalem could only complain about how difficult life was. All they could see was negativity, despair, and hopelessness because they were literally living in it. When you're surrounded by shortcomings and realize you have new restrictions, it's very easy to feel discouraged and lonely. But not Dad. I could tell that outwardly he was still his comical and considerate self, but inwardly he was processing all that had happened. Dad always sees what's going on then makes calculated decisions for everything. From football, to travel time, to financial management, to fixing things, and even to physical limitations, he's thinking of a way to fix things. He doesn't give up until it's the 4th quarter, 4th down with 0.50 seconds left in the game and it's mathematically impossible to score a touchdown. After about a day or so of learning about his new condition, he said to me,

"This is kinda messed up, ain't it."

"Yep, you're stuck in this. This is you now."

".... Always trying to keep a brotha down."

Then after a couple of more days in the hospital, Dad said "I'm going to get better and I'm going to walk again." And I believe him because Lamentations details multiple complaints, BUT God gives new mercies, morning by morning. If he believes that he will walk again, then he will.

Dad had to learn how to live a new life now. He was discharged from the hospital after confirming that his health was stable and confirmed being transferred to a rehab facility. Yep, straight from the hospital to rehab. As of now, he has not been home or even seen his house in two weeks. Once he was in rehab, therapists and nursing staff went over his daily schedule. This man has a schedule jam packed with exercises and activities that will help him at least get to 80% normalcy. He has physical therapy early in the mornings with a therapist that will teach him how to walk again and how to safely fall if needed. Then in the afternoons, he has a speech pathologist who will teach him how to take his time and swallow, pronounce his words, and correct his slurred speech. For the late afternoons, he has an occupational pathologist who will teach him how to roll over and do daily tasks independently so that he can be self-sufficient. The rehab center also teaches him how to use a wheelchair and eventually focus on just walking without distractions. He has a whole team helping him to be normal again. He gets to know his speech therapist, physical therapist, and occupational therapist well and they grow to love Dad just like everyone else. Everyday he's making progress and trying his best to make it out of rehab through the pain because his schedule wears him out! It would wear me out too if I was completely paralyzed on one side.

While Dad is in rehab, Mom, sister and I take turns visiting him every day. We just fell into a schedule where Mom would see him daily in the mornings, sister would go by after work on Mondays, Wednesdays, and Fridays, and I would go by during the evenings on Tuesdays, Thursdays, and the weekend. So, Dad saw at least one of us every day or every other day checking up on him and reviewing his progress. The first week went smoothly, but we knew it would be at least another seven weeks of rehab before we would see a great deal of his physical improvement. Eventually, the staff got to know us, and we started learning their names and their daily schedule. Even though he was in rehab, Mom was still busy bringing Dad his clothes, snacks, and medications which seemed like a full-time job. Keep in mind, she didn't trust ANY of the staff with Dad's belongings, so she was the family detective too. Time would progress and as we were glad to see Dad get better, we had to think about what's after rehab. Where will he go? What activities will he have to do?

What will insurance cover after he is discharged? What happens if he ever falls at home?

After eight weeks of rehab, we have another family consultation with Dad's therapists and medical staff about the next steps and discharge date. They go over how they'll deliver a medical bed and send him home with a wheelchair, a walker, and physical therapy exercises to do at home. They gave us direct activities to help him get in and out of the car, how he needs to get up when he falls, and exercises that he will need help with because he shouldn't be left alone while doing exercises at home. They taught us how to walk him each day to get him back to 80% functionality, but never 100%. They then tell us he cannot go back home because of the stairs, and he'll need to go to a one level living space to give him more room to be independent in a safe environment. Therefore, he must come to my new home.

"Oooooh ok, Lord. That's what all the foolishness was for. I get it now."

The Lord knew that if I had moved into my house any sooner, then I would've decorated my bonus room and turned it into my home office for my business. I would've put rugs down, had all these side tables in the way, and made it my cozy little home. That's why I went through so many delays with my closing. Unbeknownst to me, my house would be his recovery space. God knew it and he was just preparing me, preparing us for it. I bought my house right in time for his recovery and before I really started decorating it. With an open area between the dining room and family room, a huge kitchen big enough for a kitchen table with a wraparound counter to use as a brace during exercises, and a fourth bedroom to use for his medical bed, it was the perfect layout. Unfortunately, the housewarming party I had planned to have at my new house in the next couple of weeks, I cancelled it. Not postponed, CANCELLED.

Was I frustrated? Yes, because I was ready to decorate my house and my housewarming party was already scheduled. I didn't want to cancel it, but I had to and eventually just had a small get together with a handful of friends. I already mapped out what I wanted to put in each room and how my office would be decorated in the front room. I had all these plans, but I put them on hold to do what was best and the best thing was to let Dad regain his physical abilities. On the flip side, I was also grateful to even be able to buy a house that would benefit my dad. It turns out that my house was the best place for my family to be all in one space together and help take care of him while he regains some strength. All of us would rotate helping him walk, watch his physical therapy, set up things to help him be independent, and create a safe space for him. We were all under one roof.

Trust God, even when you think your problems don't make sense and you want to give up, keep trusting God. It won't make sense to you, and you will take it personally, but God has a plan for us that is not just about us. It's for the benefit of others. He's considerate of all, even when you think it's inconvenient. Even through frustration, trust the process and trust God.

Trust Him.

And we know that in all things God works for the good of those who love him, who have been called according to his purpose.

– Romans 8:28 NIV

Chapter 12: The Aftermath

My moving boxes are all unpacked and things were getting settled in. I've got my old furniture in until my new furniture arrives to fill up some of the empty space in my house. I know the color schemes I want for each room and how I want my furniture to flow. Then the medical van came. They bring in Dad's hospital bed, tools to help him walk, paperwork, andphysical therapy guides. His hospital bed was quite nice though. It had a remote control to help lift the head or foot of the bed as needed and has a lift on it to raise the bed higher if necessary. It had removable rails on the sides that helped Dad get in and out of the bed which is difficult at times since he's paralyzed on the left side now. As the medical staff is putting his bed together and showing Dad all the controls, I could tell that he doesn't have much room to roll around in his wheelchair, especially on carpet. I began to think that I complained about the original carpet being the wrong color only to realize it would end up being inconvenient for Dad while he's getting used to being in a wheelchair. Well, we had to work with what was provided for now. Hopefully this transition into my house would be smooth because after all, Dadhasn't seen his own house in over two months, and I knew he wanted to get back home.

The medical assistant finished setting up Dad's hospital bed and told us who to call for repairs or replacement parts if needed. And the key thing is to tell them when and where the bed will be placed if it is transferred to another home in the event Dad moves to a new location. Then the medical assistant leaves and goes to his next assignment.

Now for the SCHEDULES…

Two days a week, usually Mondays and Wednesdays, Dad would have a physical and occupational therapists that visited with him for one hour each to help him regain strength in his legs, teach him how to fall, how to get up off the floor, how to do daily tasks, and be more independent in this new space. They would come in and give him a good hour of exercise and walking techniques then do an assessment at the end. This would go on for at least three months, so he became familiar with the home health aides and therapists.

Then on rotation on Tuesdays and Thursdays, his speech therapist would visit him for one hour to help him talk, pronounce words, formulate sentences, and show him how to swallow again without choking. Now one of the side effects of a stroke is uncontrollable personality changes which can either make someone very mean and hostile, or very comical and silly. Well, Dad ends up being on the comical and silly side which makes him laugh uncontrollably at random times for random reasons. There are times when his speech therapist would give him sight words to say, and the words would sound too elementary or bring up a memory that would make him laugh. Imagine someone trying to help you articulate words again and all you could do was laugh in their face. And when he would get in this laughing spell all he could do was just let it run its course. It could last for one minute or ten minutes, but he would just be tickled to death about nothing. It got so bad that he kept a note card with him and whenever he started laughing, he would show people the note card until he could get himself together again. Thankfully, the therapists were understanding about it and were used to it from previous patients. As a family, we had to learn how to get used to it, but it reminded us to just laugh things off sometimes and not take life so seriously. So, he laughs! That's ok because we would rather him laugh than cuss everybody out. I don't think the same people who call my dad Barnabas could handle him randomly being angry and cussing people out, but it would've been hilarious to see. Thank God for GRACE!

The sessions spent with his speech therapists would also go on for at least three months with weekly assessments of Dad's progress. Dad's physical and mental functionality is improving, but I have a slight attitude about all these different people coming to my house throughout the week. My thoughts were, "I'm going to have complete strangers in MY house getting all comfortable and stuff when I'm not even here!! When I haven't even been in my home a full year yet!! These nurses are going to come in here and take all of my stuff right out from under me."

It took me a little time to get past the fact that not every medical person is dishonest and that the nurses were there just to support my dad and his health. Even though it felt uncomfortable having different people in my house while I'm at work, I had to remember that certain sacrifices have to be made in order to achieve the end result. Plus, I kept telling myself, "Monica…. You don't have anything for them to steal. You're STILL decorating in here. What are they going to steal…. THE CARPET!?!

I'm a very private person and really don't like a lot of people in my home, especially those I do not know or may not ever meet. So, knowing that complete strangers were coming into my home while I'm not there and while I'm still getting settled in was not comfortable for me. But I had to remember that my house wasn't about me. It wasn't just for me, but it was for my family. My house was for my family. It felt like the family home for a while and the floor plan was perfect for our situation. In my house, my dad had the bonus room up front with double doors to make it easier for him to get in and out with the wheelchair, my sister had a room, my son had a room, and I of course had the master bedroom. My mom was the only one who didn't have her own room because she would travel back and forth between my house and her house while she was moving some of Dad's belongings to my house. She liked going home to her own house on the nights that she didn't spend the night at mine. It was beneficial to have us all in the house together because we would take turns helping Dad with his therapy. On a typical weekday, my son, sister and I would leave in the mornings to school and work so we would be gone by 8:15a.m. Mom would come to my house to cook breakfast, be there when the therapists arrived, and completed some housework to make sure Dad had everything he needed for the day. My son would get off the school bus at 3:30p.m. and would help Dad with his walking exercise before starting any homework. We made sure that my son always used the guardbelt to help guide Dad on his walking path in the house and served as an extra security measure. If my dad were to fall, which rarely happened, my son was strong enough to lift him back in the wheelchair if needed. By the time they finished their exercises, Mom would leave, and I would be heading home at 5:30p.m. I would make sure my son started his homework, finish up any remaining housework then sat down to eat dinner. Dinner was always a nice, hot home cooked meal   since Mom prepared lunch and dinner for the family while we were gone. We got a little spoiled going home to a hot, good meal at the end of day, which was typically around 6:30p.m. before everyone was home again. After dinner, sister and I would check on Dad's progress, review which sessions he had left for the rest of the week, and just enjoy family time together watching a movie or playing a game. Once the day was done and everyone was settling in for the night, I would do some business work for a couple of more hours before going to sleep. Going to sleep for me meant after midnight on a good night. I was just enthusiastic about being consistent in my business while still working full time to keep a steady paycheck coming in. After all, that new mortgage payment is completely in my hands now. I'm responsible for keeping a roof over everyone's head in this house. With all of us living together it was smooth for the most part and there were only a handful of questionable instances here and there.

Instance #1

After working a long week, on Friday I decided to cook dinner and give Mom a break from the weekly duties. I got home from work around six o'clock that night and had a taste for a chicken foil pack with potatoes and vegetables and a salad for dinner. Mom was at her home resting up, so I made sure she had already eaten before I got started with dinner. Dad was ready to eat, and my son was acting like he was starving so I started dinner before sitting down because if I sit down, NOTHING will get done. I looked in my bottom cabinet to grab a pan for my foil pack and I noticed that my red stone baking pan that I've had since 2009 when I first moved out into my apartment is cracked. CRACKED??!! How? That was my favorite stone baking pan plus it came in a set. How does a stone baking pan randomly crack? My first question was "Did it happen during the move? Did a small crack grow into a bigger one and I didn't notice it until now? Who would place it back into the cabinet like nothing happened?" I knew I wasn't going crazy so instead of making accusations and interrogating everyone I decided on a plan. While I was cooking dinner, I laid the broken pan on the breakfast table in my kitchen and that way, through a process of elimination, the culprit will make themselves known. I already knew who was at fault, but I just wanted them to say something and confess to it. That's all! So, my plan would require very little work on my part to get a confession. Let the games begin! Sister was the first person to notice it. She asked, "Why is there a broken dish on your table?"

"I'm trying to figure out how it broke" I replied to her as I checked her off the list.

After dinner, my son finished his plate and brought it into the kitchen to be washed later. He saw the pan on the table.

"Hahaha. Ol' broke pan on the table looking head!!"

"And that's why you're washing the dishes tonight." Another name I got to check off the list.

We closed the kitchen for the night after my son washed the dishes, cleaned the area, and turned off all the lights. I left the pan on the table overnight for day two of the investigation. Morning comes and after Dad wakes up and completes his morning routine, he likes to go into the kitchen himself and get his own glass of water. He stays dehydrated at times; therefore he aims to drink as much water as possible during the day and avoid juice or sodas. I met him in the kitchen to start making breakfast and as he rolled into the kitchen, he noticed that the pan was still on the table.

His eye level is just a little above the table so he can't tell that the pan is broken. He said, "This pan has been out on the table all night. Should I put it up?"

"No, it's broken."

"Aw man, it's broke?"

"Yep. You know what happened to it? Did Mom mention anything about it?"

"No, I wish I knew but she didn't say anything about a pan. I'll check with her though."

"No, that's ok. Ready for breakfast?" I asked him as I mentally checked him off the list.

"Yep, whatever you're making."

I made Saturday morning breakfast and the whole house had a lazy afternoon. Saturday morning breakfast consisted of scrambled eggs, pork sausage patties, biscuits, or sometimes cinnamon rolls. After breakfast, we would take naps, watch movies, bake cookies, and go over Dad's exercises. Sister made sure that Dad wore his brace on his foot and his arm and ensured that he would walk whether he wanted to or not. She gave him grace as a daughter should but also made him exercise as a nurse should. Dad was like a live in patient and she was not going to let him wither away like other patients. There were no excuses. Dad was going to either wear the brace or wear the brace; there was no in between. On the weekends, sister and I had extra time to tend to him and be more assertive about his exercising. Dad understood the need, but sometimes he physically did not want to do them probably because he was in pain. After his exercise session and walking him around the house with the wheelchair and guard belt, we settled down for the night and prepared for church the next morning. The pan was still on the table.

Now attending church was a bit different for Dad on Sunday mornings. He's used to getting to church early because he was either singing in the choir, being a greeter, or was on program for any given Sunday. Within the manner of two months, all that has changed and he now has to have help getting dressed, tying his tie, ride with one of us to church, be wheeled into the church, and sit and enjoy service without being on duty. He enjoyed being able to attend church again, but I could tell that he missed singing in the choir or being active in the Missionary Circles. He now gets to reflect on being present and taking in the experience without being in a time crunch. After church service, we would go to Zaxby's to get a snack then head home to eat and take a good Sunday nap. Besides needing help with the buttons on his dress shirt, Dad can change his clothes easily and get into bed without any mishaps. We take our usual nap and wake up to find a movie to watch before doing exercises with Dad again. The pan is still on the table.

It's Monday morning and we're back to our normal schedule. Sister heads out to work first at 6:30a.m., then I leave to get to work by 8:15a.m. while my son leaves at the same time to catch the school bus. Dad gives us all his regular goodbye greetings before he starts his normal routine. Mom arrived shortly after to cook breakfast and confirm Dad's therapy schedule for the week along with any doctor's appointments. Usually, doctor's appointments take up most of the day with the wait time, blood work, assessments, and review of past tests to go over what's next. Then there's the prescription pick up and a late lunch to follow. Getting the wheelchair in and out of the car was the heaviest and most logistical struggle while traveling to multiple doctor's appointments. As a helpful option, medical equipment companies offer a lightweight and smaller wheelchair to travel in that makes it easier to get in and out of the car. This is beneficial for Mom since she shouldn't be lifting heavy items anyway. After completing a day full of errands, the parentals finally made it back to my house right before the rest of us got home. This time, I'm the last person to get in after attending a meeting after work that puts me home after 7p.m. Mom picked up some fried chicken from Popeye's on the way home, so I go to the kitchen to fix me a plate. I put my thigh, leg, biscuit, mashed potatoes, red beans and rice on my plate and set it down on the counter.

"Ma, what happened to my dish?"

"Ooooh…sigh…I'm just going to have to get you another one for Christmas."

"But how did it break?"

"I don't know what happened! I was taking it out of the cabinet, and it hit the counter and next thing I knew it was in two pieces. I'll get you another one. Where'd you get it from?"

"That store is permanently closed now! Lord, just tearing my stuff. Can't have nothing nice."

"I'll find you another one, child."

It took a week just for her to confess after trying to keep it a secret by placing it back into the cabinet like I wouldn't notice. Why even try to hide it?! Whew, parents!

Instance #2

With four bedrooms in my house and only two bathrooms, that meant a lot of people were sharing one bathroom. There was a synchronized schedule; sister would use the hall bathroom to get ready first since she had to be at work early before anyone else woke up; my son would then get up and start getting ready and would be done by 7:30a.m.; then my dad would be the last one to start getting ready around 8:30a.m. to occupy the bathroom. Their use of one bathroom never overlapped so there were no issues between them. I had my own master bathroom so of course I was at peace. On a Thursday, we all go through our normal morning routine and all head out to work or school, but this time Mom wouldn't be coming over to my house since she had to work. This is a rare occasion that Dad would be home alone for more than a couple of hours, but we weren't concerned since he's pretty much self-sufficient at this time and we knew his daily routine. Dad gets ready at 8:30a.m. cleaning himself up and taking his medicine with his water and sausage biscuit. I kept a second microwave on the kitchen counter so Dad could reach it and make his own breakfast or lunch by just popping meals in the microwave. After he takes his medicine, he checks his emails, listens to the news, and puts away his clothes from the laundry room. This Thursday, he has a break from the therapists coming in and he used this extra time to rest and make phone calls to family and friends.

It's late in the afternoon and I am slammed at work because I have meetings and customer appointments all day back-to-back. I barely had enough time to exhale between appointments before another customer walked in. It was crazy busy all day and by the time it's three o'clock, I'm mentally and physically burned out. I kept telling myself to make it two more hours then it'll be time to go home. I got a call from Dad towards the end of my three o'clock customer appointment and I decided to let it go to voicemail because I would call him back in about ten minutes. Then I got a call from sister which is strange because she wouldn't call me from work unless she was getting off or telling me about an event we needed to attend. Plus, I knew she was knee deep in making her rounds at work this early in the day. I ended up closing out my three o'clock appointment quickly and headed to step away to call my sister back. My manager at the time was asking if I was ready for my eighth appointment for the day, but I told him to hold on while I made a quick phone call. As I'm walking towards the break room, Dad is calling me again.

"Hey, I see you called."

"Yeah, we've got a situation here."

"You ok?"

"So, I sort of slipped in the bathroom, BUT I'M OK, I'm just stuck."

"You fell in the bathroom? You sure you're, ok?"

"No, yeah, I'm fine. I didn't fall, I just slipped off the toilet and I couldn't get up, so I needed help getting back in the chair."

"Ok, I'll head to the house and come help you."

"Well, the ambulance is on the way to help…"

"What?!"

"See I called you but didn't get through and I called your sister and couldn't get her and your mother's not answering so I pressed the button on the med alert and they're sending someone out."

"I'm leaving work now!"

"Ok, no rush. I'm here."

Dad has a way of downplaying the most important or emergency type moments. He doesn't want to cause a panic, but he does want to communicate the severity of the situation without detailing the severity of it. I literally go grab my keys and told my manager that I had to go because my dad needed help. "Ok. You coming back?"

"AM I COMING BA..." my sister's phone call interrupts me. I answered the phone and sister said, "Hey, Dad's trying to get a hold of you."

"Yeah, I just spoke with him. I'm headed to the house now."

"How did he end up on the floor?"

"I don't know but let me find out what happened."

As I'm about to finish my rant to my manager, my ring doorbell goes off letting me know someone's at my front door. It's two HEMSI paramedics and two sheriff officers. I run to the car to start heading home and I'm desperately trying to talk to the sheriffs through my ring doorbell. I wanted to let them know that I'm headed there and would be there in ten minutes. For some odd reason the microphone option on my ring app wouldn't connect so they couldn't hear me talking to them. I made sure I wasn't muted and kept trying to troubleshoot it, but they still couldn't hear me. I could hear them perfectly, but they couldn't hear me so after 48 seconds I heard them say they're breaking into my house. As I'm driving, I could literally see them using tools to bust the deadbolt out and get into the house. Eight minutes later, I made it home after passing HEMSI and the sheriff's car on my street and rushed inside only to see Dad lying down in his hospital bed. I stood there looking at him quietly, then I asked, "Are you ok?"

"Yeah, I'm fine. The medics looked me over and didn't find any bruises, scratches or broken bones. They checked my vitals, and everything looked fine."

"But you're ok?"

"Yeah, I'm better now. How are you doing?"

Still in panic mode, I simply responded with "What happened?"

"There was a little water on the floor in the bathroom and when I went to use the bathroom, my foot started to slide when I was trying to stand up and get in the wheelchair. So, it was a slow fall because I was able to brace myself using the tub, but I got stuck between the tub and the toilet. And that's when I called you."

"I'm glad you had your phone handy to call. And see, that little medical alert device that you don't like to wear came in handy, didn't it?"

"Yep, it earned its keep today. You got here pretty fast!"

"I got here."

While talking about the series of events, I got to the hall bathroom and cleaned up the water on the floor. It looks like it was left there while someone was drying off after their shower. I finished cleaning up the water then my son got off the bus and walked into the house. That's when I realized it was 4:15p.m., exactly 40 minutes after Dad had slipped. My son saw the broken lock off the door and noticed the deadbolt sitting nice and neat on the side table in the foyer. He asked what happened and I let him know the series of events that just occurred. I looked back at the door to figure out how I'm going to get it fixed so I could lock my door tonight. I'm glad the paramedics were able to come, but they sure left me with a broken lock. I always saw them breaking into homes on TV, but this real-life instance was not as entertaining. And yeah, they got to my house fast because I live at least 20 minutes away from everything in the city. I reassured my nerves by asking Dad again if he was ok and I told my son to stay in the family room until I got back from work since the front door can't be locked. I told Dad that I'm going back to work to get my purse and stuff then I'll head back home.

As I'm leaving the house, I called sister to give her an update on what happened. I told her how he slipped and how he was able to call the medics using his medical alert necklace. Before she called to talk to Dad, she reminded me to get a lock that has a keypad instead so that we could inform the medical alert team the code to get in the house in the future versus them breaking the deadbolt. That's brilliant cause I didn't even think about a keyless entry, so it made sense to have a keypad. I made it back to work and my manager expected me to literally work the last 30 minutes of the day because apparently there were people waiting for me. At this point, I didn't care who was waiting for me, I'm done for the day. Dock my paycheck or whatever because I was done for the day.

I closed out the rest of the files on my computer, locked up my desk, helped to close the vault, grabbed my purse and left. I made my way to the Home Depot store that was three minutes from my job and went looking for a new keyless entry lock for my front door. I bought an ash gray one that flushed well with my charcoal gray door, and I picked up food on the way home because there was no way I was going to cook that night. I got home and before I took my coat and shoes off, I started putting that keyless entry pad on my door. Not being able to lock my front door bothered me so I wanted to get it done quickly. I lived in a quiet neighborhood with neighbors who would watch out for each other and a watch team protecting the streets, but I still wanted to lock my door for safety and security. About 15 minutes passed and I was able to securely put the new deadbolt on and create a code that everyone in the house could remember and one that I didn't mind any medical team having access to. I told my son to try it out to make sure it was working properly. Then I conducted a mini family meeting to let them know the code and the choice of using a physical key if needed to get in the house. I told Dad that he can let the therapists and medical alert team know what the code was as needed. After our little informational meeting, I finally sat down to eat and rest. All I could think about was how today happened and what could have been done to avoid it. Dad used his resources to get him the help that he needed, but I wondered if someone always needed to be home with him. Do I need to buy rubber mats for the bathroom floor? Should we have an in-home nurse? Should I install a third bathroom with handicap accessibility? Just question after question after question ran through my mind.

Lord, thank you for your protection and strength surrounding Dad today. Continue to heal Dad as he builds his strength and endurance up. Show me. Guide me. Tell me what to do to make this recovery phase better. Cause I don't know, and I don't want to figure it out. You are greater than this situation and greater than any problem. So, move this mountain. Amen.

Instance #3

In September 2019, a category five hurricane raged through the Atlantic Ocean and caused major damage to the Bahamas and North Carolina. Hurricane Dorian appeared to have hovered over the Bahamas for a whole day while winds wereat their maximum speed of 185 mph. Areas such as Elbow Clay and High Rock of the Grand Bahama suffered the most damage with people losing homes, jobs, and some are still missing to this day. As part of the missionary programs and ministry of our church, we had a mission group that provided medical supplies, eyeglasses, and other daily necessities to other countries while also spreading the love and greatness of God is all situations. I've always wanted to be a part of a mission group because I want to help people in need in whatever circumstance they're in and show them how God still provides during the toughest situations. I just wanted to serve beyond my community and tell strangers the joy I have in the Lord even during my trials. I missed out on the last mission trip, but I was determined to make it for this one. Our church decided to help with the cleanup and repair efforts for residential homes in Bahamas especially since that was where our new pastor was born and raised. Our previous pastor had just retired, and our new pastor was barely situated in his new role by the time Hurricane Dorian happened.

The church made an announcement saying that it was decided to send a mission group to the Bahamas for one week of work that included cleanup efforts, residential home repairs, debris removal, and ministry. I did not hesitate to sign up. I'm going this time.

The informational meetings about the trip and duration started in November of 2019 with details about the cost, travel arrangements, and daily schedules for those who signed up. By the time December came around, we had our final group of six mission trailblazers ready to head to Bahamas to make an impact. Now out of a church membership of over 2,000 congregants, the fact that only six people signed up to go was surprising to me because we are a Missionary Baptist Church, but I didn't let that bother me too much. I was just glad to be going. We were scheduled to fly out in the middle of January 2020 so I had a little time to get my required shots, request time off from work, and make sure my son would have everything he needed while I was away. I was doing all this planning and had yet to tell my parents that I was officially going. I told them I was interested but didn't tell them my full desire of going because they're kind of scary. Of course, I told my sister about it first and her immediate response was "Go!" I always tell her what I'm doing first way before breaking the news to my parents. She's adventurous like I am so it doesn't take much convincing her to gain her approval. She supports me in all my decisions, except for sky diving, but that's another story for another day. By the time I got my affairs in order, get my shots, made sure my passport was still up to date, and made sure my son was ok with me leaving for a week, I finally told the parentals that I'm going on the mission trip.

Mom had the first response and asked, "Why in the world do you want to go way over there? All the way to Bahamas?"

"Yep, cause that's where the hurricane happened."

"But why?"

"I want to help repair the damage from the storm and be a witness that there's still hope even in the toughest situations."

"But you can do that here, right here at home. There's storms and tornadoes here all the time."

"Not right now though."

"So, you would rather go way over there to help people you don't know. You don't know what the conditions are over there."

"And that's why I want to go. To help. To lend a hand to those who have nothing. You can help from anywhere to everywhere."

"Lord, I don't know why my child wants to go overseas. She stresses me! And what about your son? He only has one parent?"

Even though she made a good point, my response was, "If I perish, I perish."

"Lord, let me go ahead and increase your life insurance policy because we don't know what you're getting into over there."

"I'm not going to LIVE there. It's just a week. Seven whole daysand I'll be back."

After Dad listens to the whole conversation, he summarizes it all with saying, "I can think of 1,000 reasons for you not to go, but I know you're going to go anyway."

"I'm glad you know this."

"Just be careful, ok?"

"I will be. Like, I'm coming back."

From the time I told them I was going until it was time to meet at the church to leave on our trip, Mom worried the whole time. That whole week she was worried as if I was being hauled away to some desolate city with nothing but gloom and destruction. Me on the other hand, was just as excited and determined to get this trip started. I made sure there were groceries in the house and that my son would get up on time to catch the school bus every morning like normal. I gave the parentals my travel itinerary and I let sister know the hotel we were staying in during the trip. I made sure that everything would begin like normal while I was gone. Saturday, January 18, 2020, came and it was time for our group of mission trailblazers to meet up at the church for our send off and prayer. Mom was still not happy about me going, but she ended up coming to terms with it and accepted it. We got through our hugs and goodbyes with church members who supported our willingness and desire to go and prepared to head to the airport once we checked all our supplies. All six of us loaded up in the van and made our way to the airport to start our mission. I'm full of energy and joy that I finally got a chance to make some sort of impact in someone's life, whether it be small or large.

After a week of muck and gut, mold remediation, clean up, and viewing destruction sites, it was time to head back home. Seeing damage firsthand and hearing stories of friends and family members who were still missing after Hurricane Dorian, it changed my perspective on how precious life is and how material things mean nothing. Staying in a hotel that had flood damage and walking through land where houses once stood made me realize that I was grateful to even have a home. Even though we were headed back home after a week of seeing how Bahamians lived, I kept a part of Bahamas in my memory and prayers. Nowadays I don't mind sweeping all day or figuring out how to do my own home repairs. Having everything isn't everything. Being in a different world for a week really allowed me to see how people can lose everything and still have faith in God and how people can lose everything and lose faith in God. Overall, I was ready to come home and rest.

After a long flight home with two layovers and a three-hour drive back to Alabama, the mission trailblazers all got back home at 2am on Sunday morning. After I laid down for a couple of hours, I got back up to get ready for 8:30a.m. service at church. I WAS TIRED! But it was all worth it. We had different church members approach us during and after service to see how the trip went and asked about the tasks we completed in Bahamas. One of the members was my best friend's mother who was proud of me and told me that she was glad that we made it back safely. We continued to have our conversation and she mentioned that she had a good time at my house.

I was trying not to act surprised when I said, "Oh I'm glad that you had fun."

"Yeah, you have such a beautiful house."

"Thank you! I'm still trying to decorate so things are coming together slowly."

"Oh, that's alright. Your mother did a good job hosting. She cooked dinner and everything."

"Oh, so she was hosting a get together?"

"Girl, she invited me over and she made greens, cornbread, yams, and good chicken and a dessert. I ate GOODT! We just laughed and had a good time."

"Well good! I'm glad she was a good hostess. We gotta have you back over again."

So unbeknownst to me, my mom was having parties while I'm out of town. She hadn't said a thing to me about it. Even the daily phone calls I made back home while on the trip, she never mentioned she was having a house party. Thankfully, it was my best friend's mother so she's always welcome anytime. The family and I headed home after church, and I changed clothes and just crashed. It felt like I slept for hours to physically and emotionally recover from the trip. I woke up from a long nap and told my family all the details of the trip and the things we experienced. I showed them numerous videos and pictures from the weeklong adventure and some of the people we met along with the various meals I tried. I loved eating exotic food and trying new dishes, so I was gushing over the fresh food, spices, and vegetables that Bahamians used to cook with. Sister doesn't like trying new food, so she was squirming at the daily food pictures I took while I described the taste. This made me want a snack, so I went to the kitchen and noticed that there was a huge stain on my flat top stove.

"So, Ma, you had a party while I was gone."

"Wait, she had a party?" sister said in shock.

"Yeah, you didn't know" I asked sister.

"Must've been while I wasn't here…"

Mom knew I was being dramatic when she responded, "It was just her. You make it sound like I had 20 people up in here."

"But I haven't even had my friends over yet."

"That's got nothing to do with me. Plus, she enjoyed it. We ate and had a good ole time just talking and laughing. She stayed a long time too."

"So that's why she had stuff decorated." My sister said after making a revelation.

I asked Mom, "So, what happened to the stove?"

"The pan got stuck to the stove."

"The what got stuck to the who?" I asked as if she made a mistake in her response.

"Uh, girl, I was frying chicken, so the pan got stuck a little because of the grease. It'll come out."

"She having parties while I'm gone and just messing up my kitchen. I haven't been here for a whole year yet. Can't have nothing NICE!"

Mom just sighs.

I told her, "Look, no more parties while I'm gone. No matter if I'm gone uh night or uh month, no more parties when I'm out of town. And don't tear up my kitchen. Whew Lord!"

"I'm not thinking about you."

With my whole family living under one roof, there were going to be some things that I had to get adjusted to given that all of us are grown folks. Being blessed enough to have a house that supported my family was just confirmation that when the Lord says he has mansions for you, he has riches for you…believe Him! I was literally able to house my whole immediate family in my new home comfortably! Everybody had a room. That's how God blesses abundantly. Even during tough

times, I may not like it, but he still provides everything I need. Even when I throw a tantrum.

Yes, adults have tantrums…they're just called dramatic defiance instead.

My Father's house has many rooms; if that were not so, would I have told you that I am going there to prepare a place for you?

– John 14:2

Chapter 13: Who are you convincing?

Wait, what's going on?

A pandemic?

COVID? What's that?

Oh, so this isn't just a flu-like thing, this is a REAL pandemic.

And it's shutting the whole world down. Got it!

Thank goodness we came back from the mission trip right before the pandemic happened. Two months after coming home from my mission trip in Bahamas, the world shuts down to prevent the spread of COVID-19. Now my family gets to spend a lot of time together under one roof since we're restricted from going anywhere. Our daily schedules drastically changed within a week. My son started going to school virtually. Sister still had to physically go to work because the hospital never closes; she had to wear numerous masks as an extra precaution against COVID-19. I, on the other hand, only worked three days a week on a rotating schedule at the beginning of the pandemic. One week I would only work Tuesday, Thursday, and Saturday then the next week I would work Monday, Wednesday, and Friday and so on and so on. For me, this schedule created the best work life balance by being able to do what I wanted and still receive full pay which was amazing. The extra time off between workdays led to me being more productive and organized. I used that extra time to hang out with the family, grow my business, and help my son with some schoolwork. The majority of my housework would get done in one day and I was able to cook dinner more often.

Being home more was an adjustment, but it was a good adjustment.

Sister and I had the most interaction with the public whenever we went to work so we tried to sanitize as much as possible to prevent bringing germs or illnesses home. When I came home from work, I would still have my mask on until I arrived home and went straight to my bedroom to change clothes and wash my hands. I would then sanitize all the doorknobs and counter tops as a precaution and still keep a safe distance away from the parentals. My couch would get covered in Lysol spray every night because I thought it was helping in some kind of way. Whenever sister came home, she would go straight to her bedroom. That was it. She knew that working at the hospital in the emergency room department meant that she was around every sickness, regardless of COVID-19, and she didn't want to inadvertently get the parentals sick. So, she would go straight to her bedroom and call it a night. Every day and every night it seemed like all I did was wipe down surface areas with Clorox wipes and spray furniture with Lysol. These paper towels and wipes were hard to come by during the pandemic and were getting quite expensive too along with buying masks. I ended up buying boxes and boxes of paper masks, cloth masks, and homemade masks to keep in the house, car, and at my desks at work. I had masks in various colors, sizes, and animal prints and even some with bedazzled jewels on them. I mean if I was required to wear a mask, at least make it safe and fashionable. I liked giving my masks a little personality and razzle dazzle. I did everything I could to make home life as normal as possible while still protecting everyone from sickness. Was it a stressful task? Yes, yes it was.

But at the end of the day, all I could do was clean and pray. Clean and pray.

Remember, my parents are scary. More so Mom than Dad.

Instance #4

It's a Thursday night and sister does her normal routine of coming home from work and going straight to her room. She finally gets home at eight o'clock at night after working 14 hours straight. Mom was sitting on the couch and apparently had been thinking of a plan all night and day that she thought would benefit the whole family. When sister walked in, Mom said to her, "Um, since you're around sickness all day in the emergency room I think you should change clothes in the garage or stay somewhere temporarily until all this calms down."

"Huh? Where's this coming from?"

"Well on the news, it's saying this stuff could be airborne and you're just so close to these sick people that I don't want to risk you getting one of us sick. Our immune systems couldn't handle it and Lord knows your Daddy can't get sick." Dad interrupts them by saying, "Wait, we can't single her out, now."

Now keep in mind, sister worked 12 plus hour days with the emergency room being inundated with double the normal capacity of sick patients. She had been on her feet all day, had lines all over her face from wearing multiple masks, and managed a mobile work phone that was blowing up all day with calls and texts. Working in the emergency room is a tough job already and with the pandemic raging, it had tripled the amount of workload in a matter of days. Needless to say, this is the wrong time to be having this conversation with someone who has worked non- stop to protect as many people as possible.

"That's why I go straight to my room to prevent getting anyone sick" sister replied while trying to figure out the problem.

"I don't think that's enough. We appreciate all that you do at the hospital, and I feel that they're working you too hard down there, but you're out in public and around so many people that are sick. How do we know that you're not bringing that home." I interrupted out loud and said, "We?" because I didn't know I was part of this discussion.

Sister fired back and said calmly as possible, but assertively to Mom, "So what are you suggesting?"

"Well, I think you should stay in a hotel or does the hospital have any area where you all can stay? Have them pay for a hotel for you all. Maybe they could…"

"Fine! I'll stay somewhere else."

I yelled out, "Wait! No one is leaving!"

"Nah, if she doesn't feel comfortable with me being here, I'll go." Sister then went to her room and started packing her bag. I followed right behind her to her room knowing that her mind was made up. In desperation I said to sister, "You're not leaving. The news just has her scared."

"I'm too tired to go back and forth about it."

"So, you going to let someone who doesn't own this house, make you leave?"

"YEP!"

As a family, we didn't know how bad or how long this pandemic would be and the constant news coverage of it didn't make it any better. I stopped watching the news reports on it because it was all doom and gloom. The parentals watched the news every day. They watched the news at 8am, 10am, noon, 4pm, 5pm, and until 10pm at night. And that's just the local news. They watched the national news in between the local new hours. It was just too much scary information all at one time. So, Mom felt that she was making a decision that would protect her and Dad from getting sick since both of her daughters were still interacting with the public. But she made an executive decision that negatively affected the family dynamics. In her eyes, she felt it was a reasonable request. I felt that I was losing control of my house because I am the only one that has a say in who comes and who goes. I own this house.

Once sister's mind is made up, it's made up. There's no convincing her otherwise and there's no stopping her. No matter what I said she was leaving, and she was too emotionally, physically, and mentally strained to try to argue her case further. She just wanted to lie down and go to sleep. She left that night to stay at a friend's house and I sat in my room in frustration. I kept thinking "We've got to be strong as a unit during this pandemic or else it's going to tear us apart. This house is safe, and each threshold is safe. We can't separate from each other based on fears and assumptions. After all this time, with all of us being exposed to COVID in some shape, form, or fashion, neither one of us has gotten sick. Four grown folks and a teenager living under one roof during a pandemic have not gotten sick, even with a common cold, in months! Is that not God! Isn't that God's grace!"

The mood in the house was different for the rest of that week. I was quiet cause I let a disturbance happen in my house. Dad was still trying to resolve the matter between Mom and sister and kept checking up on sister to see how she was doing. My son kept asking "is auntie back yet?" Mom kept reiterating that she didn't mean to hurt anyone's feelings and that she just wanted us to all be safe. At this point, I'm realizing that one decision or one action from one person affects the whole household, so my main goal was to fix the situation. That's what I am, I fixer. I will find a million ways to fix a situation as strategically as possible. The hardest part would be to work around emotions to achieve the best desired outcome. It's been two nights so far and having my sister out of the house is not sitting well with me. I called her up to see what she was doing.

"Sister! What are you doing?"

"Just leaving work. Is she there?"

"Nope, she's gone back home."

"I'll come over there and get some more clothes later."

"Girl, just come on back. It makes no sense for you to be in different places. Plus, I'm making spaghetti."

"Oh spaghetti! I'll be there long enough to get some stuff."

"Just gone on and stay when you come. It'll be alright."

On Sunday night, sister came by after work to get some more things. Yes, she worked seven days a week during the height of the pandemic. When she came over, she saw that Dad and I were still in pajamas and asked how church service went. The church house was closed too so church services were virtual now and Dad and I had been home all-day watching TV. While we talked about Dad's schedule for the week, I showed sister the pot of spaghetti that was hot and ready. She started to head to her room, and I told her to just sit and eat first. We talked while she ate, and I told her that going back and forth was too much and living out of a bag didn't make sense. She said, "I'll just make sure I'm not here when she's here." Fine, whatever. My thoughts were to get the house back in order without any more discourse. It took a while, but eventually sister was back home, and Mom did her daily run back and forth to my house without any disagreements. Not every disagreement ends with an apology and sometimes things tend to fall back into place without addressing the issue. Trying to mix five different personalities under one roof was hard and it required prayer, patience, and forgiveness to get through inconveniences and influences. Sometimes it takes patience first to deal with situations, prayer to get through it with understanding, then forgiveness after realizing that people see things from their own perspective. No one else.

Finally, there's peace in the house.

Instance #5

Out of all of us, Mom does the most traveling between my house and their house. Mom spends about three nights a week at my house and stays four nights at her house. She brings Dad his extra clothes and medications and on the days she was not at my house, she was either working, running her own errands, or attending meetings. She had to manage their household bills, their appointments, household chores for their house, and cook dinner every other night. This is a new role for her with having to manage everything and it started to get tiresome. She wanted things to be back to normal, but unfortunately, this was the new normal now. Change happens even when we're not prepared because it occurs at the most inconvenient time.

My house is 20 minutes away from the parentals house, which is not bad, so I go to their house from time to time when Mom is there to complete some minor repairs that she needs. Usually, it's minor repairs like repainting a room, fixing internet issues, replacing fluorescent tubes, or fixing the TV. I'm not a cable guy but for some reason my parents need their cable fixed for what seems like every six weeks. And they can never remember their passwords for anything. I had to reset their passwords for the phone, internet, email accounts, and computer login then write them in their password book along with keeping it in my phone just in case. Basically, I'm their geek squad and handyman that they like to call on at the last minute. Imagine keeping passwords for two different people living in two different houses and each with four different accounts. That's a lot to keep up with, not including my own personal stuff. To make it simple, I downloaded an app that securely saves online account information and passwords in one simple space, and it allows me to create ID cards for each person and each account. I'm able to add notes to it, documents, and reminders as needed to help me stay on track with everything. Because if it's not in my calendar or in the app, then it's not getting done. Occasionally, sister and I take Dad by their house to see it, gather some things, and have a few date nights with Mom there. It's been almost two years now since Dad had his stroke and he's only seen his house about eight times during that time frame. When we do take him over there, he can only see the lowest level downstairs since he can't get up the stairs in the house or the ones leading to the front porch. Every time he enters his house, he wants to badly go upstairs. He rolled his wheelchair to the bottom of the stairs and made mental calculations of how to physically get up the stairs. I stood in the background quietly just watching his mind think out loud about the various ways to conquer the stairs. After a few minutes, he backed his wheelchair up and turned it around to face me and said, "I'm getting up those stairs." I responded with "Ok" not in disbelief, but in acceptance that if he says and believes he will one day get up the stairs again then he will do it. He accepted defeat for now, but it stays in the back of his mind. Whenever Dad has a physical limitation, he constantly thinks of ways to overcome them. I learned that he doesn't want to be stuck with a disability nor feel like he's a burden to us. I know that he wants to walk again. He knows I want him to walk again. I've even dreamed numerous times about him walking so it had to become a reality again, right? He's going to walk me down the aisle one day, right?

Because of the constant back and forth between houses, Mom starts suggesting that Dad moves back home. She felt it would be better for him to be home to cut down some of the travel logistics. We listened to her idea then sister and I suggested that they should downsize first before moving Dad back home. Lord why did we say that! Through Mom's ears, it sounded like we told her to leave her country and move way across the world. We suggested downsizing because their house had now become too big for the two of them to maintain; they shouldn't be climbing any stairs; there's two sets of stairs in the house which makes it harder to transport someone in and out of the house; their utility bill is too high; and they need to have a one level home. Sister told Mom that Dad needed to be in a home where he has enough space to move around in the wheelchair and manage his dependency. I told Mom that selling their home would include any equity they've obtained and can use those funds to go towards a smaller home in the same neighborhood and still have funds left over to live off of for at least a couple of years. I reiterated that it would be less maintenance, lower household bills, and easier access to the house. We kept telling them that neither one of them needed to be climbing any stairs AT ALL. After all these suggestions, Mom doesn't want to sell her house. We asked, "why not?" She said, "I like my house. It's close to everything and we have so many memories in this house. Then having to pack everything up is just too much. It's easier just to move him there."

Then sister said, "You would stay in the same neighborhood just in a smaller house all on one level. It doesn't make sense to have the stairs."

"Then where would family stay when they visit?"

"Ma, when was the last time someone spent the night over there, like more than one night. Ain't nobody staying over there! Not THAT often" as I pointed out the obvious. Sister tried to convince her that "It would just be easier on the both of you to get a smaller house. Downsize."

"Nope! I like the house I'm in."

We ended that conversation and started going over how to manage tasks better to relieve Mom of repetitive duties. I would chip in to take Dad to his appointments whenever I had slow days at work. Sister would do more exercises with him at night to continue building up Dad's strength. After completing his virtual schoolwork, my son would make sure Dad ate something while waiting for one of us to come home and cook. We had a plan of how all this would work out and continued rotating tasks between each of us. For another year, we would manage trips to doctor's appointments, picking up medications, maintaining the parental's house, find resources to extend home healthcare, and made sure Dad had all his medical equipment including a motorized chair.

A year has passed, and Mom brings up the conversation of Dad coming home again, but this time there's no backing down. She's tired of the back and forth. Tired of being in the house by herself. Tired of figuring things out by herself. Tired of always having a bag packed to spend the night. She's tired. We understand her frustration, but we want to make sure his move back home is safe and beneficial for everyone. Sister and I gave her the steps to get rid of some furniture and clothes in the house and speak with a realtor about putting their house on the market. We tell Mom to consider the houses for sale in my neighborhood or the two for sale in her neighborhood. We go through a timeline for these tasks, but all she could hear was more things she had to do. Out of frustration, Mom told us "I don't want to move. I want to stay in my house. Why can't we just move your father home?" Again, sister told her "Because he doesn't have much space to move around or do his exercises. He needs to be in a one level house and so do you. Just listen to us on this."

"He'll have space to move around, and he'll have clear access to the downstairs bathroom and computer area."

"That bathroom has a washer and dryer in there. It's too tight of a space for the wheelchair to fit."

"We'll get a smaller wheelchair."

"Where are you going to put his bed?"

"I'll move the couch to the computer area so we can fit his bed in the den by the fireplace. I've already measured it, and it will fit."

"How's he going to make his own food?"

"I'll put a mini fridge and microwave downstairs."

I chimed in by asking, "How's he going to shower? I have a walk-in shower that he's been using here."

"I'll have one built downstairs for him since you didn't get a handicap shower during the build."

I quickly responded with "I didn't know I was building a house for this…Look, long-term wise and for the improvement of his health, sell the house and downsize. Dad has been able to build his strength up and be more independent here and we don't want to slow that process down. He has access to everything on all one floor here and it gives him enough space to move around. So, again, sell the house then use that money to buy a smaller house in your neighborhood for a cheaper price and still be close to everything. Use any extra money to live on and we'll make new memories in the new house. That's the plan."

"So, your house is better than mine?"

"That's not what she's saying. Functionality wise, he's better off in a one level home" as sister comes to my defense.

"So, you would rather..." and Mom cuts me off by yelling "I would rather stay in my house!"

This conversation went on for another hour and all I could do was sit back and listen from now on because the hardest thing to do is to convince my parents to sell one of their prized possessions and assets and move. Mom's mind is made up and we can talk until we're blue in the face but that won't change anything. What sister and I think is that this conversation is going in one ear and out the other. The more sister, Dad, and Mom talked about it, the more I realized it was not about the house. It was about the fact that they don't want to give up a major part of their life to accommodate a change they didn't ask for. They don't want to be told when and how to leave their house. They don't want to be told that the life they had was no longer theirs. They don't want to let go of 40 plus years of hard work and determination because their children think it'll be better to change their entire living arrangement. They don't want to be told what to do.

Dad noticed that I had been quiet for a while and said, "You've been quiet over there, what do you think about it?"

"Go home…. I've told you all my thoughts and suggestions on what I think is best, but you all are grown and you're going to do what you want to do. So go home. I've said my peace."

One thing I will not do is go back and forth with grown folks. I don't like going back and forth on anything really. But I'm definitely not going to talk in circles about something that is going to continuously upset the whole family. If my parents want to both be back in their own homes, then God's speed. It's not about me and my suggestions. It's about them and their lives and I can't live it for them.

Bear with each other and forgive one another if any of you has a grievance against someone. Forgive as the Lord forgave you.

– Colossians 3:13 NIV

Chapter 14: So Let It Be Written, So Let It Be Done

Two weeks after the discussion about Dad moving out of my house, Mom prepares their house for his bed. Mom has moved the couch from the den downstairs over into the next room which is the computer room. She has bought a mini fridge for Dad's water bottles and juices and placed a microwave on top for his breakfast entrées and snacks. There's a half of step between their den and computer room so Mom has purchased a rubber mat that will help Dad maneuver his wheelchair easier between rooms. She has placed a new faucet and bathroom organizer in the downstairs bathroom so Dad can have easier access to his toiletries throughout the day and night. She has even bought him new pajamas and a side table to keep his Bible and water handy next to his bed. She was so excited to have him back home soon. I asked her, "So you just wanted your man back home with you?" and she just smiled back at me. She told me that she already informed his therapists about the new address to come to for his sessions and has displayed emergency contact numbers for them just in case they need it. She was ready for him to come home after three years at my house.

The weekend comes and we all chip in to get Dad moved back home. I was responsible for taking down Dad's hospital bed and making sure all the parts stayed together. My son managed moving his furniture like his chest, small side table, eating tray and mattress. Sister made sure all of Dad's clothes were packed up and cleared out of his closet and drawers. We started that morning and by the afternoon, we had packed up Dad's clothes, shoes, bed, drinks, snacks, and medical supplies. We loaded everything up between my car, sister's car, Mom's car, and a neighbor's car that came over to help with the move. We put Dad in Mom's car last and headed to their house. Once we were there, I unloaded Dad's bed and started putting it back together like it was before and made sure his controls were working well. We put his clothes in the drawers of his knee-length dresser, so he has access to them whenever he wants and filled up his mini fridge with water bottles and juices. We get everything set up just the way he had it at my house, but in a smaller room. Even though sister and I don't like our parent's decision, we all work together smoothly to get Dad moved back into his home. He's glad to be home and see it for more than a few hours. He likes having access to his own computer again and has already figured out how he can still do his exercises. It's nighttime and we've checked to make sure everything has been moved in and Dad is comfortable back in his new, old space. We let our parents know that if they needed anything to just call us, but we'll keep checking on him daily like normal. We discussed how they'll need to call us if he has to be home alone for a long period of time so we can check on him and bring him something to eat. We looked everything over one more time before sister, son, and I headed back home. As we're walking out, Dad rolled up behind us and said, "Well, I'm all moved in now, so I guess I'll be here."

Sister responded with "Yep! It'll be different but you're home, right?" in a sarcastic voice. I then said jokingly, but seriously, "And there's no coming back to my house."

We said our goodbyes and we headed home. Even though they can take care of themselves, sister and I just can't fathom how this situation is going to turn out. We'll still take care of him and her, but we know that it'll be extra work for Mom since it's just her with him majority of the time compared to four of us being there with him. We don't feel confident about it, but there's nothing we can do now besides respect their wishes. Arriving back home, my house feels a bit different now, a little empty. I started to vacuum Dad's room and reorganize the closet to put my coats and business supplies in. What Dad's room was just hours ago slowly transformed into my office. I stood in that room for a little while to imagine what color I wanted to paint the walls, think about all the nights that Dad sat there and read his Bible, and how things changed so quickly. Now it was time for the next chapter of my life. Week after week, I added more things to my office. First, I painted a wall in my office an ocean blue color to match my business colors. It took me a week to paint it because I had to measure my lines for the diamond pattern accent wall that I wanted. I wanted my office to have a little pizzazz.

Next, I started ordering a work desk and a bookshelf to place some décor and awards on to remind myself of where I had been in business and prepare for where I was going. Then came the filing cabinet, worktable, storage bench and office chairs. Little by little, my office started to come together like I had planned before my father's stroke. A minor sacrifice wasn't that bad since God blessed me with the space for my Dad to recover. Waiting to decorate my office wasn't as inconvenient as I thought it would be. But part of me felt bad for decorating my office because it felt like I was preventing a way for my Dad to come back. I soon realized that was the goal; for him to not have to come back. That he would improve so much that he would be coming back to visit and not have to stay. My house served its purpose for that time and now I get to do what I want in my house. In my home. In my safe space.

There were things I learned about myself and caregiving while he lived with me that completely strengthened my relationship with God because I know who He is for me. One of the most important lessons I learned was how the fruits of my spirit helped to make being a caregiver more bearable.

LOVE

I have real love for my family. I would flip the world upside down to protect and do what's right for them. Love is truly an unconditional action and way of thinking that continues to grow through various situations. Showing love as a caregiver meant enduring things side by side with my parents that I couldn't control. It meant not just seeing illness as it was presented but seeing the fight to triumph over things working against us. I had to see the worst and the best of my parents and have enough love to know that they were going through life just like I was and sometimes they didn't know what to do. I had to love them harder on the days when they were just trying to stay alive. Love is action. Love is forgiveness. Love is understanding. Love is deep.

PEACE

When I was younger, I learned that it was pointless to ask God why things were happening. The why was no longer important to me after seeing both of my parents endure cancer and the lifelong diseases that followed. God is sovereign and He does what He wants to do so me asking why was not going to change the situation. All I asked was that the Lord show me what I'm supposed to learn, what behavior am I supposed to change, or what characteristic was I supposed to gain. Lord, just sit next to me and show me who I'm supposed to be after all of this because it must amount to something. Sickness cannot be their life or my life. So, learn me the way because whatever my lot, whatever their lot, whatever our lot, it is well with my soul because Lord you are here. How do I know? Because we, as a family, have survived everything and with that I have peace in every valley.

KINDNESS

There were times when my parents got on my nerves! They seemed to be so needy. But every time they called; I was there for them. I wanted to help them, take care of them, and make sure they were ok physically and mentally. I wanted to do for them what they would've done for me. Their sickness was not who they would be even if they had a little attitude about it. Knowing that we are each other's responsibility is what helped me to stay present for them within my boundaries. Being available was a kind gesture of love towards my parents. Setting my own boundaries to limit how much of my time I would dedicate to them was a form of kindness extended to myself. I can't be everything to everybody all the time, but I can be my best self to do what's important at the right time. Caregiving is a hard role, so I learned to be kind to myself first to be kind to others.

FAITHFULNESS

My parents did not want to be sick, and they weren't expecting it either. For Mom, it went from breast cancer, to diabetes, then heart disease within a span of 20 years. For Dad, it was pneumonia, to Multiple Myeloma, to prostate cancer, then three strokes within the same 20 years. The faith that my parents have in God never wavered. I remember seeing my mom still pray on her knees every night whether she was in pain or not. Dad reads his Bible every night even if he was in the hospital. Their faith never shook, but it stayed a solid foundation for their hope, healing, and strength. I know who God is for them and I came to understand why their faith remained strong. I know who God is for me and that's why my faith grows stronger every year.

I don't know how I juggle being a single mother, a full-time entrepreneur, a helpful daughter, a supportive sister, an annoying aunt, an active church member, and a dedicated friend, but I aim to accomplish it with grace. These are the priorities that I keep at the top of my list so everything else just had to wait. When you know what's important to you because it brings the greatest value to your life, you make time for it. So, I'm faithful over these few things because they amount to be the greatest asset in my life. I'm faithful over a few things.

SELF-CONTROL

There were times when I was angry. I was angry at my parents for not taking me to the movies in high school because they were tired and didn't want to drive there and back. I was angry at the doctor because he couldn't figure out why I passed out. I was angry at the medical staff for telling me I had to be sanitized before seeing my dad. I was angry at a church member for living their life. And I was also angry at my parents for not downsizing. I was angry, but I never acted out. I just kept clinching my fist as an immediate reaction and played racquetball in my spare time as a therapeutic hobby. I kept my thoughts and actions reserved for the proper time while secretly flipping tables in my mind. I've always been observant and had control over my feelings, which is a strength and a weakness. It's a strength because my actions could change a situation drastically for unnecessary reasons and yet I don't let them define me; but it's a weakness because there have been times when I'm literally screaming inside, and no one can tell. Stressed out to my core, but no one can tell. Filled with sadness, but not one tear falls. Why? Because I control my feelings. Why? Because I ask God to manage it because my frame is too small to carry this burden and therefore, I will not carry this burden. I have self-control because I let God lead and guide my actions.

My Peace to You

Being a caregiver is a role that is placed upon without preparation and without sufficient warning. You're having to care for someone while caring for yourself and managing the other aspects of your life. It can quickly take over your life and physically drain you. It will also affect your mental health and make you question things that are out of your control. So, try to take it one day and one battle at a time. There's no right or wrong way to be a caregiver and there's no champion status for it either. You're not doing it for any recognition or to help you feel better about yourself. But you're doing it because your loved one needs someone to fight for them and with them through every sickness. Be there to lift them up in need and genuinely care about their physical well-being. There will be times where they want to give up and other times when they'll want to run a marathon. Just be there on the roller coaster with them and help them have a quality, dignified life. However, you do it, do it with love. And remember that you have a life outside of caregiving and it's ok to live it without feeling selfish.

Whenever a caregiver tells me their loved one passed, I never say "Oh, I'm sorry to hear that" because sometimes there is healing on the other side of through. Instead, I tell them, "I know they appreciated you taking care of them and helping them enjoy life. You were good caregiver, and they will always be proud of you because you helped them live as long as they did, with grace."

My joy, my hope, and my faith will make you forget I went through something for so long.

RESOURCES

Here are resources personally used by the author that were beneficial during the caregiving journey for the loved one and the caregiver. There is no blueprint or a guide to caregiving so the author hopes that these resources will be a guide during each aspect of caregiving.

For medical supplies, such as wheelchairs, walkers, shower chairs, hospital beds, etc.

McAbee Medical Inc.
304 Governors Dr., SW
Huntsville, AL 35801
(800) 729-9817
Mcabeemedical.com

For In-Home Healthcare and medical solutions:

Aveanna Healthcare
400 Interstate North Parkway, SE
Ste. 1600
Atlanta, GA 30339
(770) 441-1580
Aveanna.com

HALO Home Care
250 Sun Temple Dr.
Ste. C5
Madison, AL 35758
(256) 325-5023
Homecarehalo.com

For counselling and therapy to navigate through mental health issues:

A Better Way Counseling and Consulting
(215) 616-2053
Abetterwaycc.com

For eco-friendly aromatherapy candles that help to relieve stress and induce relaxation:

Affirmare Candle Co.
affirmarecandle.com

For assistance with neuropathy, back pain, neck pain, blood circulation, etc.

Max Health
5000 Whitesburg Dr.
Ste. 140
Huntsville, AL 35802
(256) 212-0937
Maxhealthal.com

www.ingramcontent.com/pod-product-compliance
Lightning Source LLC
Chambersburg PA
CBHW020333010526
44119CB00002B/52